Better Homes and Gardens®

GOOD FOOD ON A BUDGET

For an elegant meal on a budget, serve roasted Rice-Stuffed Chicken. This appetizing dish starts with money-saving chicken, rice, and tomatoes. As a thrift and flavor bonus, you use the chicken livers in the stuffing.

On the cover: Here's a menu that offers family-sized servings without a strain on your pocketbook. Feature herb- and apple-flavored Individual Pot Roasts, plus Whole Wheat-Bran Rolls and Easy Orange Sherbet.

BETTER HOMES AND GARDENS BOOKS
Editorial Director: Don Dooley
Managing Editor: Malcolm E. Robinson   Art Director: John Berg
Food Editor: Nancy Morton
Senior Food Editor: Joyce Trollope
Associate Editor: Nancy Byal
Assistant Editors: Sharyl Heiken, Lorene Mundhenke,
Sandra Mosley, Pat Olson
Copy Editor: Lawrence Clayton
Designers: Julie Zesch, Harijs Priekulis ·

CONTENTS

HOW TO CUT FOOD COSTS

BUDGET-TRIMMING MENUS

MONEY-SAVING MAIN DISHES

ECONOMICAL SIDE DISHES

MORE FOR YOUR MONEY

INDEX

Our seal assures you that every recipe in *Good Food On A Budget* is endorsed by the Better Homes and Gardens Test Kitchen. Each recipe has been tested for family appeal, practicality, and deliciousness.

HOW TO CUT FOOD COSTS

"Every time I go to the store, my grocery bill goes up." This statement is made daily by homemakers throughout the country. More than likely, you have said the same thing. It's little wonder you feel this way. First of all, food costs do keep rising. Sometimes, they reflect the cost of seasonal foods, but all too often they indicate a new level of prices.

And second, to complicate matters, large food markets offer 8,000 to 10,000 attractive items that often tempt you to forget costs and to indulge in impulse buying.

Your challenge is to keep spending within a budget without lowering the quality of the food you buy. And that's what this book is all about. It's geared to help you 'think economy' by using a well-organized plan, good shopping habits, and proper preparation techniques. This approach to budgeting combined with the menus and recipes in this book will help you to provide good food on a budget and, at the same time, cut food costs by as much as 20 percent.

PLANNING

To accomplish this goal, you must first have a plan. Start by analyzing how much you now spend on the various food items. Do this by keeping an accurate spending record for the next week or two. With this information, you can decide what and how many changes to make in your buying habits.

Then, to decide what to buy, create delicious and nutritious daily menu plans for several days or a week at a time (see Budget-Trimming Menus, pages 6-37, and the Basic Four Food Guide, page 87). Admittedly, this may take half an hour or more each week, but the financial savings (hundreds of dollars a year) more than pay for the added time you spend planning.

Start planning your menus with the main dishes, since the largest part of the food dollar is spent on meat. Turn to pages 90-91 for help in selecting meats. These meats plus poultry and fish generally give you more per serving at less cost. Also read food store advertisements in the newspaper for the specials that can be used in main dishes. And for a budget-bonus, occasionally substitute less expensive meat alternates such as dry beans or peas for meat.

Besides meat, plan to use other bargains that the store advertises. Fit these into the remaining parts of the menus as side dishes, salads, and desserts, being sure to fulfill the requirements of the Basic Four.

Now that your menu plans are complete, convert these plans into a shopping list. From the recipes, list the ingredients plus the form and amount that you need to purchase at the store (see How Much to Buy chart, front cover). Also check the cupboard to see what staples you are low on. (Make it a habit to replace staples when they are on sale.) Finally, to save time later, reorganize the list into the order that you will see the foods at your food store.

SHOPPING

With the above list, you're on your way to successful budgeting. However, you also must be a wise shopper to achieve total economy.

Although you should stick to your shopping list, be on the alert for unadvertised store specials that are genuine bargains. To recognize bargains, compare the 'sale' price with what you normally pay (see Unit Price Chart, back cover). For example, learn to identify a loss leader — by selling the food at a sale price, the store takes a loss in the hopes you will do more shopping. Take advantage, too, of seasonal sale foods (lower in cost during peak production periods) as well as 'cents off' promotions.

For additional control, take along a purse-sized adder to total your purchases as you select them. If the total nears your spending limit, check the foods on your list as well as those already in the shopping cart to see what unnecessary items you can omit.

PREPARING

Proper use of food once it is purchased can also help you save on food costs. If your handling techniques are poor, the planning and shopping will be to no avail. To avoid food waste, get the food home, unpacked, and stored under the proper conditions immediately (see page 89). Use perishable foods during their peak of quality so there will be little, if any, to throw away. Utilize all edible parts of food. For example, remove only thin layers of peel, and carefully separate inedible portions. Finally, turn a small amount of leftovers into real dividends by adding them to casseroles, salads, soups, and the like (see leftover recipes and chart, pages 70-71).

PROOF IN DOING

Now that you see how easy it is to cut the food bill, get out a pad and pencil and begin to plan. Besides using the above cost-cutters, be sure to consult the More For Your Money section (pages 84-92) to develop a budget strategy. Incorporate the menus and recipes that follow — all designed with economy in mind — into your meal plans. Also make note of the money-saving tips throughout the book, set off by a dollar sign economy symbol. After a few weeks of serving flavorful and attractive foods, you'll be convinced that the money-wise habits have made your life easier and your savings significant.

BUDGET-TRIMMING MENUS

Does the food bill seem to climb higher and higher no matter how hard you try to cut your spending? Then, maybe you're bypassing one of the most important steps toward successful budgeting—considering the *total* costs of every meal.

This section of appealing, yet low-cost menus helps you to accomplish this task. Included are menus and the accompanying recipes for family dinners, lunches (including boxed lunches), and breakfasts, as well as special-occasion and company meals that you can prepare. For those who need to budget both money *and* time, there are quick-to-make, low-cost menus, too. By using these appetizing, nutritious meals, you'll take the doldrums out of budgeting, and, at the same time, serve your family an interesting variety of good-tasting and hearty foods.

Please meat-and-potato fanciers with this outdoor menu featuring Barbecued Chili Steak, Herby Grilled Potatoes, and Creamy Coleslaw.

FAMILY DINNERS

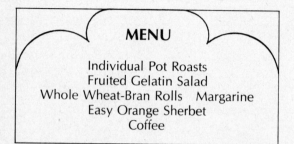

Besides being a good buy, beef pot roast continues as an all-time family favorite. Give the pot roast (shown on the cover) a new twist by cutting the meat into individual servings before you cook it. For added savings, make homemade rolls and sherbet.

WHOLE WHEAT-BRAN ROLLS

     1 package active dry yeast
 1½ cups stirred whole wheat flour
     1 cup reconstituted nonfat dry milk
 ¼ cup shortening
 ¼ cup sugar
     1 teaspoon salt
     1 egg
 ½ cup whole bran
 1½ cups sifted all-purpose flour

In large mixer bowl combine yeast and whole wheat flour. Heat milk, shortening, sugar, and salt just till warm, stirring occasionally. Add to mixture in bowl; add egg. Beat at low speed with electric mixer for ½ minute, scraping sides of bowl constantly. Beat 3 minutes at high speed.

By hand, stir in bran and enough all-purpose flour for a soft dough. Mix well. Place in greased bowl, turning once. Cover; let rise till double. Punch down; turn out on floured surface. Let rest 10 minutes. Shape into 24 balls; place in greased muffin pans. Let rise till double. Bake at 400° for 10 to 12 minutes. Makes 24.

INDIVIDUAL POT ROASTS

     1 2-pound beef arm pot roast
     2 beef bouillon cubes
 ¼ teaspoon garlic powder
     1 small bay leaf
 ⅛ teaspoon dried thyme leaves,
        crushed
     6 medium carrots, peeled and bias-
        cut in 1½-inch pieces (2 cups)
     1 cup applesauce
     1 medium onion, sliced
     1 large apple, cored and sliced
     2 tablespoons cornstarch
 ½ teaspoon Kitchen Bouquet (optional)

Trim excess fat from meat; remove bone. Cut meat in 4 pieces. In Dutch oven heat fat trimmings till 2 tablespoons fat accumulate; discard trimmings. Brown meat. Season with 1 teaspoon salt and ⅛ teaspoon pepper. Dissolve bouillon cubes in ½ cup boiling water. Add bouillon, garlic, bay leaf, and thyme to meat. Cover; cook slowly 1 hour. Add carrots, applesauce, and onion. Cover; cook till tender, 1 hour.

Add apple; cook about 10 minutes. Remove meat, vegetables, and fruit to warm platter. Skim off fat from pan drippings. Combine cornstarch and ¼ cup cold water; add to drippings. Cook and stir till thickened and bubbly; cook 1 minute. Stir in Kitchen Bouquet. Makes 4 servings.

EASY ORANGE SHERBET

Pour 1 cup evaporated milk into freezer tray; freeze till ice crystals form around edges. In small bowl whip milk till stiff peaks form. Beat in one 6-ounce can frozen orange juice concentrate, thawed, and ⅓ cup sugar. Tint orange with red and yellow food coloring. Turn into large freezer tray. Freeze till nearly firm, 1 to 2 hours. Stir. Freeze till firm. Makes 1½ quarts.

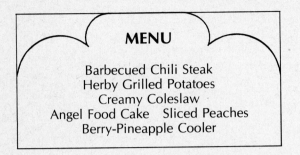

MENU

Barbecued Chili Steak
Herby Grilled Potatoes
Creamy Coleslaw
Angel Food Cake   Sliced Peaches
Berry-Pineapple Cooler

Even if you are on a budget, you can have your steak and eat it, too. Try this low cost, flavorful chuck steak with other outdoor classics—grilled potatoes and coleslaw—as pictured on page 6.

CREAMY COLESLAW

    3 cups shredded cabbage
⅓ cup finely chopped onion
½ cup salad dressing or mayonnaise
    1 tablespoon sugar
    1 tablespoon vinegar
½ teaspoon salt
½ teaspoon celery seed
    1 small green pepper, cut in rings
       (optional)

Combine cabbage and onion. Blend salad dressing, sugar, vinegar, salt, and celery seed. Pour over vegetables and toss. Top with green pepper. Makes 6 servings.

BERRY-PINEAPPLE COOLER

    1 envelope unsweetened strawberry-
       flavored soft drink powder
    1 cup sugar
    6 cups cold water
    1 18-ounce can unsweetened
       pineapple juice (2¼ cups)
    Crushed ice

Combine soft drink powder and sugar. Add water; stir till soft drink powder and sugar are dissolved. Stir in pineapple juice; chill. Serve in chilled glasses filled with crushed ice. Makes 8 cups.

HERBY GRILLED POTATOES

¾ cup margarine or butter
¼ cup finely chopped celery
    1 teaspoon dried oregano leaves,
       crushed
½ teaspoon salt
¼ teaspoon garlic powder
⅛ teaspoon pepper
    6 medium potatoes
    2 medium onions, thinly sliced and
       cut in half crosswise

In saucepan melt margarine. Add celery; cook till tender. Stir in oregano, salt, garlic powder, and pepper. Cutting not quite through, slit potatoes into ½-inch slices. Place each potato on a piece of foil large enough to wrap potato.

Drizzle *about half* of margarine mixture into slits. Insert a half slice of onion into each slit. Drizzle with remaining margarine. Bring edges of foil together; seal securely with double fold. Grill over *hot* coals 40 to 45 minutes. Makes 6 servings.

BARBECUED CHILI STEAK

½ cup vinegar
½ cup catsup
    2 tablespoons cooking oil
    2 tablespoons finely chopped onion
    2 teaspoons chili powder
    1 teaspoon salt
⅛ teaspoon pepper
    3 pounds beef chuck steak, cut 1½
       inches thick

Combine first 7 ingredients. Slash fat edges of meat. Place in shallow dish. Pour vinegar-catsup mixture over steak. Let stand 3 hours at room temperature or overnight in refrigerator, turning steak several times. Drain steak, reserving marinade; pat dry with paper toweling.

Cook over *hot* coals about 20 minutes on each side for rare, or 25 minutes on each side for medium. Brush occasionally with the reserved marinade. Carve meat across grain in thin slices. Makes 6 servings.

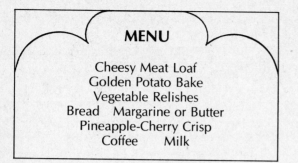

MENU

Cheesy Meat Loaf
Golden Potato Bake
Vegetable Relishes
Bread   Margarine or Butter
Pineapple-Cherry Crisp
Coffee   Milk

Two old favorites, meat loaf and mashed potatoes, are featured in this appetizing meal. For a new look as well as a boost in both flavor and nutrition, add cheese to the meat loaf and use carrots in the potato dish. To complete the meal, serve crisp relishes, bread, the fruit crisp for dessert, and your choice of coffee or milk.

PINEAPPLE-CHERRY CRISP

1 16-ounce can pitted tart red
    cherries, drained
1 8¾-ounce can crushed pineapple,
    undrained
1 cup granulated sugar
2 tablespoons quick-cooking tapioca
1 tablespoon lemon juice
    Few drops red food coloring
• • •
1 cup sifted all-purpose flour
1 cup quick-cooking rolled oats
⅔ cup brown sugar
½ cup margarine or butter, melted

In medium saucepan combine drained cherries, undrained pineapple, granulated sugar, quick-cooking tapioca, lemon juice, and red food coloring. Let stand 15 minutes; cook and stir till thickened and clear, 5 to 10 minutes. Cool.

Mix together flour, rolled oats, brown sugar, and melted margarine or butter. Press *half* the crumb mixture into a 9x9x2-inch baking pan. Spread pineapple-cherry filling over. Top with remaining crumb mixture. Bake at 350° for 30 minutes. Cut into squares; serve warm. Makes 9 servings.

CHEESY MEAT LOAF

½ cup chopped onion
¼ cup chopped green pepper
1 8-ounce can tomato sauce (1 cup)
2 beaten eggs
4 ounces process American cheese,
    diced (1 cup)
1 cup soft bread crumbs (1¼ slices)
1 teaspoon salt
    Dash pepper
¼ teaspoon dried thyme leaves,
    crushed
1½ pounds ground beef
½ pound ground pork

Cook vegetables in boiling water till tender; drain. Stir in remaining ingredients *except* meat. Add meat; mix well. Shape into loaf in baking dish. Bake at 350° for 1½ hours. Makes 8 to 10 servings.

GOLDEN POTATO BAKE

2 pounds potatoes, peeled (about 6
    medium potatoes)
1 16-ounce can diced carrots,
    drained, or 2 cups diced carrots,
    cooked and drained
    Hot reconstituted nonfat dry milk
2 tablespoons margarine or butter
    Salt and pepper

Cook potatoes in boiling, salted water till tender; drain. Add carrots. Mash at low speed with electric mixer; slowly beat in enough milk to make light. Stir in margarine and a little salt and pepper. Turn into a 2-quart casserole. Dot with additional margarine, if desired. Bake at 350° for 25 minutes. Makes 8 servings.

Menu magic

Ground meat and potatoes, long noted for their →
economy and versatility, are the supper standouts
for Cheesy Meat Loaf and Golden Potato Bake. If the
budget allows, garnish meat with pickled peppers.

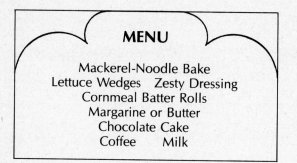

MENU

Mackerel-Noodle Bake
Lettuce Wedges   Zesty Dressing
Cornmeal Batter Rolls
Margarine or Butter
Chocolate Cake
Coffee   Milk

The goodness of homemade foods such as noodles, salad dressing, and rolls is emphasized in this family-pleasing menu. And, as an added bonus, these delicious dishes are all inexpensive to prepare.

ZESTY DRESSING

¾ cup salad oil
¼ cup vinegar
2 tablespoons sugar
1 teaspoon grated onion
1½ teaspoons Worcestershire sauce
½ teaspoon salt
½ teaspoon chili powder
¼ teaspoon garlic powder
1 hard-cooked egg, finely chopped

In screw-top jar combine all ingredients *except* hard-cooked egg. Cover and shake. Chill. Shake again just before serving. Stir in egg. Makes about 1 cup dressing.

HOMEMADE NOODLES

1 beaten egg
2 tablespoons reconstituted nonfat dry milk or fluid milk
1 cup sifted all-purpose flour

Mix egg, milk, and ½ teaspoon salt. Add enough of the flour to make stiff dough. Roll very thin on floured surface; let stand 20 minutes. Roll up; cut in ¼-inch slices. Spread out; dry 2 hours. Drop noodles into boiling, salted water. Cook, uncovered, about 10 minutes. Drain.

MACKEREL-NOODLE BAKE

1 cup chopped celery
½ cup chopped onion
1 16-ounce can peas, drained, or
    1 10-ounce package frozen peas, cooked and drained
1 15-ounce can mackerel or 1
    16-ounce can pink salmon, drained, bones and skin removed, and flaked
1 15-ounce can tomato sauce
    Homemade Noodles
2 ounces process American cheese, shredded (½ cup)

Cook celery and onion in 2 tablespoons water, covered, till tender, 5 to 7 minutes. Combine with next 4 ingredients, ¾ teaspoon salt, and ⅛ teaspoon pepper. Turn into a 2-quart casserole. Bake at 350° for 30 minutes. Top with cheese; bake 5 minutes. Makes 6 to 8 servings.

CORNMEAL BATTER ROLLS

1 package active dry yeast
5 cups sifted all-purpose flour
2¼ cups reconstituted nonfat dry milk
½ cup shortening
½ cup sugar
1 tablespoon salt
2 eggs
1 cup yellow or white cornmeal

In a large mixer bowl combine the yeast and 3½ cups of the flour. Heat the next 4 ingredients just till warm, stirring occasionally. Add to dry mixture in mixer bowl; add eggs. Beat the mixture at low speed with electric mixer for ½ minute, scraping the sides of the bowl constantly. Beat 3 minutes at high speed.

By hand, stir in cornmeal and enough remaining flour to make a soft dough. Cover; let rise in warm place till double. Stir batter down; fill greased muffin cups ⅔ full. Cover; let rise in warm place till double. Bake at 400° till golden, 15 to 20 minutes. Makes 2 dozen.

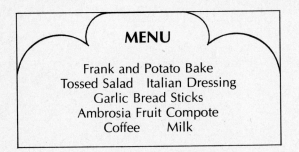

Include frankfurters on your list of foods that offer great eating pleasure for little money. They're flavorful, versatile, and don't contain one bit of waste.

FRANK AND POTATO BAKE

1 pound frankfurters
⅔ cup reconstituted nonfat dry milk
1 tablespoon all-purpose flour
8 ounces process cheese spread, cut up (2 cups)
2 tablespoons minced onion
2 teaspoons finely snipped parsley
8 medium potatoes, cooked, peeled, and sliced (8 cups)

Reserve 3 franks; slice remaining franks and set aside. In saucepan stir milk into flour till smooth. Add cheese; cook and stir till thickened and smooth. Add onion, parsley, and ½ teaspoon salt; fold cheese mixture into potatoes and sliced franks. Turn into a 2-quart casserole. Bake, covered, at 350° for 40 minutes. Halve reserved franks; arrange in pinwheel atop casserole. Bake, uncovered, 10 minutes. Top with parsley, if desired. Makes 8 servings.

GARLIC BREAD STICKS

Combine ½ cup softened margarine and ½ teaspoon *each* garlic powder and paprika. Trim crusts from 8 slices white bread, if desired. Spread both sides of bread with margarine. Cut each slice into four sticks. Place on baking sheet. Bake at 350° for 10 to 15 minutes. Makes 8 servings.

AMBROSIA FRUIT COMPOTE

2 medium oranges, peeled
1 17-ounce can whole, unpitted purple plums, drained
1 13½-ounce can pineapple tidbits
¼ cup brown sugar
½ teaspoon rum flavoring
¼ cup shredded coconut

Grate ½ teaspoon orange peel; set aside. Section oranges, reserving juice. Halve and pit plums. Drain pineapple, reserving ¼ cup syrup. Combine fruits and orange juice. Heat pineapple syrup, brown sugar, and orange peel till sugar dissolves. Stir in rum flavoring. Pour over fruits. Stir; chill. Garnish with coconut. Serves 8.

For a change from hot dogs and buns, try this cheese-sauced Frank and Potato Bake. Since the meat and potatoes are in one dish, you only need a tossed salad, bread, and beverage for accompaniments.

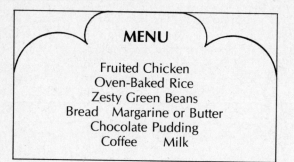

MENU

Fruited Chicken
Oven-Baked Rice
Zesty Green Beans
Bread   Margarine or Butter
Chocolate Pudding
Coffee   Milk

Always popular and low-cost, chicken takes on an attractive look when it's baked in a pineapple sauce. Baked rice, green beans, and your favorite chocolate pudding are just-right accompaniments.

OVEN-BAKED RICE

1½ cups uncooked long-grain rice
3¾ cups hot water
¼ teaspoon salt

Toast long-grain rice in skillet over medium heat, shaking often, about 20 minutes. Turn into a 1-quart casserole; add water and salt, stirring to separate rice. Cover and bake at 350° till rice is tender, about 1 hour. Makes 8 servings.

ZESTY GREEN BEANS

1½ cups ½-inch bread cubes (2 slices)
2 tablespoons margarine or butter
2 16-ounce cans cut green beans,
    drained, or 2 10-ounce packages
    frozen green beans, cooked and
    drained
2 tablespoons vinegar
1 tablespoon margarine or butter
2 teaspoons minced onion
½ teaspoon salt

Cook bread cubes in 2 tablespoons margarine till crisp and golden. Set aside. In saucepan heat beans with remaining ingredients. Stir in the bread cubes just before serving. Makes 8 servings.

FRUITED CHICKEN

¾ cup sifted all-purpose flour
¼ teaspoon each salt, garlic salt,
    celery salt, and ground nutmeg
2 2½- to 3-pound ready-to-cook
    broiler-fryer chickens, cut up
½ cup margarine or butter
1 20-ounce can pineapple tidbits
3 tablespoons all-purpose flour
1 tablespoon sugar
⅓ cup soy sauce

In a bag mix ¾ cup flour and seasonings. Add chicken pieces, a few at a time. Shake to coat. Brown chicken in margarine. Place in 13½x8¾x1¾-inch baking dish, reserving drippings. Drain fruit, reserving 1 cup syrup. Arrange fruit over chicken. Stir 3 tablespoons flour and sugar into drippings. Add syrup and soy; cook and stir till thickened and bubbly. Spoon over meat. Cover; bake at 350° for 1 hour. Serves 8.

POULTRY SAVINGS

When buying chicken and turkey, use these tips to tuck away extra cents:
● Select whole birds rather than cut-up ones, and cut them yourself (see page 92).
● Buy several chickens when there's a special. Cut and sort like pieces, then freeze packages of breasts, legs, etc.
● Choose one large bird in preference to two smaller ones. The big one provides more meat and less bone and fat per pound.

Hints of the East

The soy- and pineapple-flavored sauce in Fruited → Chicken is reminiscent of foods prepared in oriental kitchens. To give the meal an added foreign overtone, include Oven-Baked Rice.

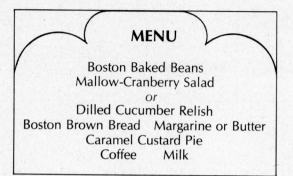

MENU

Boston Baked Beans
Mallow-Cranberry Salad
or
Dilled Cucumber Relish
Boston Brown Bread   Margarine or Butter
Caramel Custard Pie
Coffee   Milk

Follow the tradition established by New England colonists of serving hearty, yet thrifty food by preparing baked beans and brown bread for Saturday night supper. As an added bonus, the ingredients for the main part of this meal are easily assembled. Then your range top and oven take over for the long, slow cooking that helps develop full flavor in the bread and beans.

BOSTON BROWN BREAD

    1 cup sifted all-purpose flour
    1 teaspoon baking powder
    1 teaspoon baking soda
    1 teaspoon salt
    1 cup yellow or white cornmeal
    1 cup whole wheat flour
    2 cups sour milk*
    1 cup raisins
    ¾ cup dark or light molasses

Sift together first 4 ingredients; stir in cornmeal and whole wheat flour. Add sour milk, raisins, and molasses; beat well. Divide the batter among 4 greased and floured 16-ounce fruit or vegetable cans. Cover tightly with foil.

Place cans on rack in deep kettle; add boiling water to depth of 1 inch. Cover; steam bread for 3 hours, adding more boiling water if needed. Uncover cans; cool 10 minutes. Remove bread. Wrap; store overnight before serving. Makes 4.

*Combine 2 tablespoons lemon juice or vinegar with enough sweet milk to make 2 cups; let stand for 5 minutes.

BOSTON BAKED BEANS

    2 cups dry navy beans (1 pound)
    ½ cup dark or light molasses
    ⅓ cup brown sugar
    1 teaspoon dry mustard
    ¼ pound salt pork, cut in half
    1 medium onion, chopped

Rinse beans; add to 2 quarts cold water. Bring to boiling; simmer 2 minutes. Remove from heat. Cover; let stand 1 hour. Add ½ teaspoon salt. Cover; simmer 1 hour. Drain, reserving liquid. Measure 2 cups liquid, adding water if needed; mix with molasses, sugar, and mustard. Score *half* of salt pork; grind remainder. In 2-quart casserole combine beans, ground pork, and onion. Pour sugar mixture over. Top with scored pork. Cover; bake at 300° for 5 to 7 hours. Add liquid, if needed. Serves 8.

MALLOW-CRANBERRY SALAD

Dissolve one 3-ounce package raspberry-flavored gelatin in 1 cup boiling water. Stir in one 16-ounce can whole cranberry sauce. Chill till partially set; fold in ½ cup chopped celery. Pour into 6½-cup ring mold; chill *almost* firm. Soften 1 envelope unflavored gelatin in ½ cup cold water; dissolve over low heat. Beat in ½ cup salad dressing, ⅔ cup evaporated milk, and 1 tablespoon lemon juice. Chill till partially set; whip till fluffy. Fold in 1 cup miniature marshmallows. Pour over berry layer; chill till firm. Makes 8 servings.

MONEY-SAVING MEAT ALTERNATIVES

Occasionally, substitute dry beans, peas, and lentils for meat. These vegetables are economical sources of protein, and they give your menus tasty variety.

DILLED CUCUMBER RELISH

   2 tablespoons salt
   2 medium unpeeled cucumbers,
      thinly sliced
   1 small onion, chopped (⅓ cup)
   ⅔ cup vinegar
   ¼ cup sugar
   ½ teaspoon celery seed
   ½ teaspoon dillweed
   ¼ teaspoon garlic powder
   ¼ teaspoon dry mustard

Combine ½ cup water and salt; pour over cucumbers. Let stand 30 minutes; drain and rinse. Combine cucumber and onion. In saucepan combine ⅔ cup water and remaining ingredients; bring to boiling. Pour over vegetables; chill. Makes 2¾ cups.

CARAMEL CUSTARD PIE

   1 14½-ounce can evaporated milk
   2 eggs
   1 cup brown sugar
   3 tablespoons all-purpose flour
   2 tablespoons margarine or butter
   1 unbaked 9-inch pastry shell (See
      page 83)

Add enough water to evaporated milk to make 2 cups; beat in eggs. Combine brown sugar and flour; cut in margarine till mixture is like coarse crumbs. Add milk mixture to brown sugar mixture; beat till well blended. Pour into pastry shell. Bake at 400° till knife inserted halfway between center and edge comes out clean, about 30 minutes. Cool thoroughly.

Re-create the irresistible aromas that filled early New England kitchens by preparing Boston Baked Beans and raisin-studded Boston Brown Bread. Bake the bread a day ahead to allow the flavors to mellow.

COMPANY DINNERS

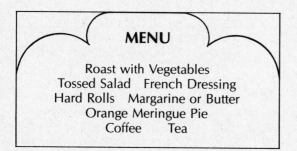

MENU

Roast with Vegetables
Tossed Salad   French Dressing
Hard Rolls   Margarine or Butter
Orange Meringue Pie
Coffee   Tea

If company's coming and you want to serve a special meal that's economical, try this menu. A little fancier cut of meat than usual, a distinctive gravy, and a cream pie stand out as being company-special, yet budget-minded dishes.

ORANGE MERINGUE PIE

    ¾ cup sugar
    ¼ cup cornstarch
    ¼ teaspoon salt
  1½ cups orange juice
    2 slightly beaten egg yolks
    1 tablespoon margarine or butter
    1 teaspoon grated orange peel
        (optional)
    1 baked 8-inch pastry shell (See
        page 83)
    2 egg whites
    ¼ cup sugar

In saucepan combine ¾ cup sugar, cornstarch, and salt. Slowly stir in juice. Cook and stir till thickened and bubbly. Reduce heat. Cook 1 minute more; remove from heat. Stir small amount of hot mixture into yolks; return to hot mixture. Cook and stir 2 minutes more. Stir in margarine and peel. Pour into pastry shell.

Beat egg whites to soft peaks. Slowly beat in ¼ cup sugar to stiff peaks; spread over hot filling, sealing edges. Bake at 400° for 7 to 9 minutes. Cool on rack.

ROAST WITH VEGETABLES

    1 4-pound rolled beef rump roast
    ⅛ teaspoon each dried marjoram
        leaves, crushed, and dried thyme
        leaves, crushed
    8 medium potatoes, peeled and
        halved
    8 medium carrots, peeled and cut up
        Herb Gravy

Place meat, fat side up, on rack in shallow roasting pan. Combine ¼ teaspoon salt, herbs, and dash pepper; rub into meat. Roast at 325° till meat thermometer registers 150° to 170°, about 2 to 2½ hours.

Meanwhile, in separate saucepans cook potatoes and carrots in boiling, salted water 15 minutes; drain. About 45 minutes before roast is done, place vegetables in drippings around roast, turning to coat. When done, remove meat and vegetables; keep warm. Sprinkle vegetables with snipped parsley, if desired. Use pan drippings for Herb Gravy. Serves 8 to 10.

Herb Gravy: Pour meat juices and fat into large measuring cup. Skim off fat, reserving 3 tablespoons. Add water to juices to make 2 cups; set aside. Return reserved fat to pan. Stir in ¼ cup all-purpose flour; cook and stir over low heat till blended. Remove from heat. Add meat juices all at once; blend. Stir in 1 tablespoon snipped parsley, ¾ teaspoon salt, dash pepper, dash *each* crushed dried marjoram leaves and crushed dried thyme leaves. Cook and stir till thickened and bubbly. Simmer 2 to 3 minutes.

A special look and taste

For an elegant dinner, serve Roast with Vegetables →
and melt-in-your mouth Orange Meringue Pie. To
highlight the main dish, surround the rolled rump
roast with parsley-topped potatoes and carrots.

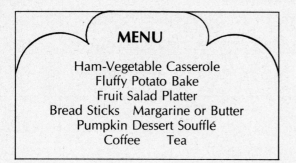

MENU

Ham-Vegetable Casserole
Fluffy Potato Bake
Fruit Salad Platter
Bread Sticks   Margarine or Butter
Pumpkin Dessert Soufflé
Coffee   Tea

Trying to hold down the cost of entertaining? A flavorful, colorful casserole makes the ideal main dish. You make the meat, the most costly part of the meal, go farther by adding such foods as sauces, vegetables, pasta, rice, or bread. Then, on a buffet table surround the casserole with several simple, yet tempting accompaniments.

PUMPKIN DESSERT SOUFFLÉ

A light and fluffy meal capper—

      1 cup evaporated milk
   ¾ cup brown sugar
      2 envelopes unflavored gelatin
   ¼ teaspoon salt
   1½ cups canned pumpkin
      3 slightly beaten egg yolks
   ½ teaspoon ground cinnamon
   ½ teaspoon ground nutmeg
   ¼ teaspoon ground ginger
      3 egg whites
   ½ cup granulated sugar

Pour evaporated milk into freezer tray; freeze till soft ice crystals form around edges. Meanwhile, in saucepan combine brown sugar, gelatin, and salt. Stir in 1¼ cups cold water, pumpkin, egg yolks, and spices. Cook and stir over low heat till thickened and bubbly. Remove from heat; chill till partially set.

Beat egg whites to soft peaks. Slowly add granulated sugar, beating to stiff peaks. Fold into pumpkin. Whip icy milk till stiff; fold in. Turn into a 2-quart soufflé dish; chill till firm. Serves 12.

HAM-VEGETABLE CASSEROLE

   ½ cup chopped onion
   ¼ cup margarine or butter
   ⅓ cup all-purpose flour
   ½ teaspoon salt
      Dash pepper
      1 tablespoon prepared mustard
   1½ teaspoons Worcestershire sauce
      1 16-ounce can tomatoes, cut up
      1 14½-ounce can evaporated milk
      4 cups cubed, fully cooked ham
      3 10-ounce packages frozen mixed
         vegetables, cooked and drained,
         or 3 16-ounce cans mixed
         vegetables, drained
   1½ cups soft bread crumbs (2 slices)
      2 tablespoons margarine or butter,
         melted

In saucepan cook onion in ¼ cup margarine till tender but not brown. Blend in flour, salt, pepper, mustard, and Worcestershire sauce. Add tomatoes and milk. Cook and stir till thickened and bubbly. Remove from heat; stir in ham and vegetables. Turn into a 13x8¾x1¾-inch baking dish. Combine bread crumbs and melted margarine; sprinkle atop casserole. Bake at 350° about 30 minutes. Serves 12.

USE UP EXTRA FRUIT SYRUP

Save the syrup that you drain from canned or frozen fruits and use it in any one of the following ways:
● Replace part of the water with syrup when making gelatin salads or desserts.
● Thicken the syrup with cornstarch for meat glazes or dessert sauces.
● Make dressings to accompany fruit salads by combining fruit syrup with salad dressing or mayonnaise.
● Flavor and sweeten your favorite milk or fruit drinks by using fruit syrup.

FRUIT SALAD PLATTER

> 1 17-ounce can whole, unpitted
> purple plums
> ¼ cup sugar
> 2 tablespoons cornstarch
> ¼ teaspoon ground cinnamon
> 1 tablespoon lemon juice
> 5 drops red food coloring
> ½ cup salad dressing or mayonnaise
> 1 16-ounce can pear halves, chilled
> 4 oranges, chilled
> Lettuce

Drain plums, reserving syrup; chill plums. Add water to syrup to make 1½ cups. Combine sugar, cornstarch, and cinnamon; blend in syrup. Cook and stir till thickened and bubbly. Cook 1 minute. Stir in lemon juice and food coloring. Cool; blend in salad dressing. Chill thoroughly.

At serving time, drain pears. Peel and section oranges; drain. Arrange plums, pears, and oranges on lettuce-lined platter. Serve with dressing. Makes 12 servings.

FLUFFY POTATO BAKE

A tangy version of mashed potatoes—

> 3 pounds potatoes (6 large)
> ¼ cup finely chopped onion
> ¼ cup margarine or butter
> 1 12-ounce carton small curd cream-
> style cottage cheese (1½ cups)
> ¼ cup snipped parsley
> 1 teaspoon salt
> Margarine or butter, melted
> (optional)

Cook, peel, and mash the potatoes. In a saucepan cook onion in ¼ cup margarine till tender but not brown. Stir onion, cottage cheese, parsley, and salt into mashed potatoes. Spoon potato mixture into a well-greased 2-quart casserole. Drizzle melted margarine over top, if desired. Bake at 350° till mixture is heated through and browned, about 30 minutes. Garnish the potato casserole with additional snipped parsley, if desired. Makes 12 servings.

Remember this buffet menu next time you're considering what to serve for company. Feature bread crumb-topped Ham-Vegetable Casserole for the main course plus Fluffy Potato Bake and Fruit Salad Platter.

LUNCHES TO EAT AT HOME

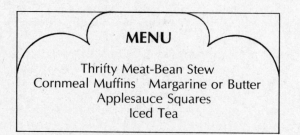

MENU

Thrifty Meat-Bean Stew
Cornmeal Muffins   Margarine or Butter
Applesauce Squares
Iced Tea

Couple luncheon meat with lima beans and you create an inexpensive stew that's the focal point for a noon menu. You only need to add muffins, dessert, and a beverage to round out the meal perfectly.

THRIFTY MEAT-BEAN STEW

    1½ cups large dry limas (12 ounces)
    3 cups cold water
    1 16-ounce can tomatoes, cut up
    ¼ cup chopped onion
    ½ teaspoon salt
        • • •
    1 12-ounce can luncheon meat, cubed
    1 beef bouillon cube
    ⅛ teaspoon pepper
    1 cup reconstituted nonfat dry milk
        or fluid milk
    3 tablespoons all-purpose flour
    1 teaspoon Kitchen Bouquet (optional)

Rinse beans; place in large saucepan and add water. Bring to boiling; cover and simmer 2 minutes. Remove from heat and let stand 1 hour. (Or add beans to water and soak overnight.) *Do not drain.* Add tomatoes, onion, and salt; cover and simmer for 1¼ hours. Add luncheon meat, bouillon cube, and pepper. Bring to boiling; reduce heat and simmer 15 minutes, stirring occasionally. Combine milk and flour; add to stew mixture. Cook, stirring constantly, till thickened and bubbly; stir in Kitchen Bouquet. Makes 8 servings.

APPLESAUCE SQUARES

    1½ cups applesauce
    ¼ cup brown sugar
    2 tablespoons all-purpose flour
    1 tablespoon lemon juice
    ½ cup margarine or butter
    ½ cup brown sugar
    ½ cup all-purpose flour
    1 cup quick-cooking rolled oats
    ½ cup shredded coconut
    ½ teaspoon ground nutmeg

In saucepan combine first 4 ingredients. Cook and stir till thick and bubbly. Cool.

Cream margarine and ½ cup brown sugar. Mix in ½ cup flour and ¼ teaspoon salt; stir in oats. Press *half* the oat mixture into 8x8x2-inch baking pan. Spread cooled filling over crust. Add coconut and nutmeg to remaining oat mixture; sprinkle over filling. Bake at 375° for 30 to 35 minutes. Cool; cut in squares. Serves 8 or 9.

CORNMEAL MUFFINS

Sift together 1 cup sifted all-purpose flour, ¼ cup sugar, 4 teaspoons baking powder, and ¾ teaspoon salt; stir in 1 cup yellow or white cornmeal. Add 2 eggs, 1 cup reconstituted nonfat dry milk, and ¼ cup shortening. Beat with rotary beater or electric mixer just till smooth. (Do not overbeat.) Fill greased muffin pans ⅔ full. Bake at 400° for 20 to 25 minutes. Makes 12 to 14 muffins.

Hot meal for cold weather

When the thermometer dips below zero, this trio of →
foods will be a welcome sight. Serve slow-simmered, Thrifty Meat-Bean Stew with warm-from-the-oven Cornmeal Muffins and Applesauce Squares.

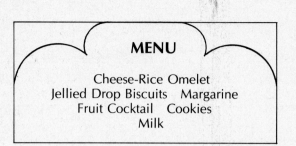

MENU

Cheese-Rice Omelet
Jellied Drop Biscuits   Margarine
Fruit Cocktail   Cookies
Milk

A fancy egg main dish perks up the lunch menu and works wonders on the pocket-book as well. This flavorful oven-going omelet is enhanced by rice and cheese, plus a zesty tomato sauce served over it.

CHEESE-RICE OMELET

   1 10½-ounce can condensed tomato
     soup
  ½ cup reconstituted nonfat dry milk
  ¾ teaspoon chili powder
  ½ teaspoon onion powder
  ⅛ teaspoon pepper
  4 egg whites
  ½ teaspoon salt
  4 egg yolks
  ½ cup cooked or leftover rice
  4 ounces sharp process American
    cheese, shredded (1 cup)
  1 tablespoon margarine or butter

In saucepan blend soup with milk; stir in chili powder, onion powder, and pepper. Heat through, stirring occasionally.

Meanwhile, beat whites till frothy; add 2 tablespoons water and salt. Beat till stiff. Beat yolks till thick and lemon-colored. Fold yolks, rice, and cheese into whites. Heat margarine in 10-inch oven-going skillet. Pour in eggs; spread evenly, leaving sides higher. Reduce heat. Cook, uncovered, till set, 8 to 10 minutes.

Place skillet in oven. Bake at 325° till knife inserted in center comes out clean, about 10 minutes. Loosen sides of omelet. Make shallow cut across omelet slightly above and parallel to skillet handle. Tilt pan. Fold smaller half over larger. Slip onto platter. Spoon on sauce. Serves 4.

JELLIED DROP BISCUITS

Make an impression in each biscuit, then fill with your favorite jelly—

  2 cups sifted all-purpose flour
  4 teaspoons baking powder
  2 teaspoons sugar
  ½ teaspoon salt
  ½ teaspoon cream of tartar
       • • •
  ½ cup shortening
  ¾ cup reconstituted nonfat dry milk
    or fluid milk
  ⅓ cup jelly

Sift flour, baking powder, sugar, salt, and cream of tartar into mixing bowl. Cut in shortening till mixture resembles coarse crumbs. Make a well in dry ingredients; add milk all at once. Stir quickly with a fork just till mixed.

Drop biscuit dough from tablespoon onto greased baking sheet. Make a thumbprint in the top of each biscuit; fill each center with some jelly. Bake at 450° till browned, 10 to 12 minutes. Makes 16.

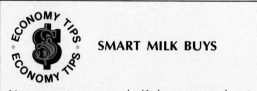

SMART MILK BUYS

You can save over *half* the money that is normally spent for milk by using the following suggestions:
● Keep a constant supply of reconstituted nonfat dry milk in the refrigerator for cooking and drinking. If your family prefers a richer product for drinking, mix equal parts of fluid whole milk and reconstituted nonfat dry milk.
● Make use of evaporated milk in cooking, too. To substitute it for fluid milk, combine equal portions of the milk and water.
● Purchase milk products from the grocery store, since a home delivery service is usually more costly.

MENU

Grilled Beef Sandwiches
Dill Pickles   Cherry Tomatoes
Baked Rice Pudding
Rosy Iced Tea

Sandwiches are a welcome sight to children and adults alike. These inexpensive ingredients give the old favorites an appetizing new look and taste.

GRILLED BEEF SANDWICHES

   2 tablespoons prepared horseradish
      Dash pepper
   ½ cup margarine or butter,
      softened
        • • •
   12 slices white bread
   12 thin slices cooked or leftover
      roast beef
   6 ounces process Swiss cheese, sliced
      (6 slices)

Stir horseradish and pepper into margarine or butter. Spread on *both* sides of each slice of bread. Top *half* the slices with roast beef, cheese, then remaining bread. Over medium-low heat brown the sandwiches on both sides on a griddle or in a skillet till cheese melts. Makes 6 servings.

ROSY ICED TEA

   3 cups freshly brewed tea
   3 cups cranberry juice cocktail
   ¼ cup light corn syrup
   3 tablespoons lemon juice
      Ice cubes
      Lemon wedges (optional)

Combine tea, cranberry juice cocktail, corn syrup, and lemon juice. Pour over ice cubes in tall glasses. Garnish with lemon wedges, if desired. Makes 6 servings.

BAKED RICE PUDDING

Tastes good warm or chilled—

   3 beaten eggs
   2 cups reconstituted nonfat dry milk
      or fluid milk
   ½ cup sugar
   1 teaspoon vanilla
   ½ teaspoon salt
   1¾ to 2 cups cooked or leftover rice
   ⅓ to ½ cup raisins (optional)
      Ground nutmeg

Combine first 5 ingredients; mix well. Add rice and raisins. Turn into 10x6x1¾-inch baking dish. Bake, uncovered, at 325° for 30 minutes; stir. Sprinkle with nutmeg. Bake till knife inserted halfway between center and edge comes out clean, about 30 minutes more. Serves 6.

Turn leftover roast beef into a flavor treat. For Grilled Beef Sandwiches spread bread slices liberally with a zesty horseradish-margarine mixture, then sandwich beef and Swiss cheese in between.

LUNCHES TO CARRY

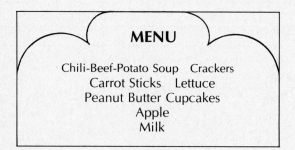

MENU

Chili-Beef-Potato Soup   Crackers
Carrot Sticks   Lettuce
Peanut Butter Cupcakes
Apple
Milk

Portable lunches needn't always be cold. Use a widemouthed vacuum jar to keep foods such as nutritious soups and stews steaming-hot until lunchtime.

PEANUT BUTTER CUPCAKES

½ cup brown sugar
½ cup sifted all-purpose flour
¼ cup peanut butter
2 tablespoons margarine, melted
½ teaspoon ground cinnamon
• • •
½ cup peanut butter
⅓ cup shortening
1½ cups brown sugar
2 eggs
• • •
2 cups sifted all-purpose flour
2 teaspoons baking powder
½ teaspoon ground cinnamon
½ teaspoon salt
1 cup reconstituted nonfat dry milk

Combine first 5 ingredients till crumbly; set aside. Cream ½ cup peanut butter and shortening. Slowly beat in brown sugar. Add eggs, one at a time, beating till fluffy. Sift together flour, baking powder, cinnamon, and salt; add alternately with milk, beating after each addition. Fill paper bake cups in muffin pans half full. Top with crumbly mixture. Bake at 375° for 18 to 20 minutes. Makes 24 cupcakes.

CHILI-BEEF-POTATO SOUP

½ pound ground beef
½ cup chopped onion
½ cup chopped celery
1 16-ounce can tomatoes, cut up
2 cups diced, peeled potatoes
1 10½-ounce can condensed beef broth
1 soup can water (1⅓ cups)
1 teaspoon chili powder
½ teaspoon salt
½ teaspoon Worcestershire sauce
1 cup cooked or leftover peas or
   green beans

Brown meat in large saucepan. Drain off fat. Add onion and celery; cook till vegetables are crisp-tender. Stir in tomatoes, potatoes, beef broth, water, chili powder, salt, and Worcestershire sauce. Cover and cook till potatoes are tender, about 15 minutes. Stir in peas or beans; heat through. Makes 6 servings.

HOLD DOWN THE COST OF LUNCH

Prepare a packaged lunch for the business-man and woman as well as the school children in your family. They'll appreciate the foods' home-cooked taste, and enjoy being dollars ahead, too.

Lunch-box pleasers

Chili-Beef-Potato Soup with crackers and Peanut Butter Cupcakes are sure to appeal to either a child's or an adult's hungry appetite. Relishes, milk, and an apple complete this well-balanced meal. →

BREAKFAST BRIGHTENERS

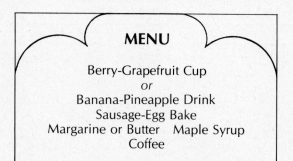

MENU

Berry-Grapefruit Cup
or
Banana-Pineapple Drink
Sausage-Egg Bake
Margarine or Butter   Maple Syrup
Coffee

Serve either the fruit cup or the fruit beverage as the first course for this menu. Then, bring on the Sausage-Egg Bake. Making this dish for breakfast provides a pleasant change and is also a budget-minded way to stretch sausage and eggs.

SAUSAGE-EGG BAKE

½ pound bulk pork sausage
1 cup sifted all-purpose flour
2 tablespoons sugar
4 teaspoons baking powder
½ teaspoon salt
1 cup yellow or white cornmeal

• • •

2 eggs
1 cup reconstituted nonfat dry
    milk or fluid milk
3 hard-cooked eggs, chopped

Brown bulk pork sausage slowly in skillet; drain, reserving ¼ cup drippings. Set aside. In mixing bowl sift together all-purpose flour, sugar, baking powder, and salt; stir in yellow or white cornmeal. Add the 2 eggs, reconstituted nonfat dry milk, and reserved drippings. Beat with rotary beater just till smooth. Fold in browned sausage and chopped hard-cooked eggs. Pour into greased 9x9x2-inch pan. Bake at 425° till done, 20 to 25 minutes. Serve warm. Makes 6 to 8 servings.

BERRY-GRAPEFRUIT CUP

1 cup sugar
2 cups cranberries
3 grapefruit, peeled and sectioned

In saucepan combine sugar and 1 cup water; stir to dissolve sugar. Heat to boiling; boil 5 minutes. Add cranberries; cook till skins pop, about 5 minutes more. Remove from heat; chill. Pour cranberry mixture over grapefruit sections in individual serving bowls. Makes 6 servings.

BANANA-PINEAPPLE DRINK

2 cups unsweetened pineapple juice,
    chilled
1 large, fully ripe banana, cut up
    Ground nutmeg

Place juice and banana in blender container; cover. Blend till smooth. Pour into juice glasses. Garnish with nutmeg. Serves 6.

MAPLE SYRUP

1 cup light corn syrup
½ cup brown sugar
    Dash maple flavoring
1 tablespoon margarine or butter

Combine syrup, brown sugar, and ½ cup water; cook and stir till sugar is dissolved. Stir in flavoring and margarine.

Old-time flavor

Serve Berry-Grapefruit Cup and generous slices of →
Sausage-Egg Bake for a breakfast that tastes like you spent hours in the kitchen. Top the sausage-and-egg corn bread with margarine and Maple Syrup.

MENU

Spicy Oranges 'n Prunes
Butterscotch Oatmeal
or
Chicken-Rice Scrapple
Tea

Here's a fruit and cereal breakfast that's sure to start the day off right both nutrition- and money-wise. Either version of cooked cereal will be a sure hit.

SPICY ORANGES 'N PRUNES

    12 whole cloves
     1 11-ounce can mandarin orange
        sections
     8 ounces unpitted dried prunes

Tie cloves in cheesecloth. Drain oranges, reserving syrup. In saucepan combine syrup, 1½ cups water, prunes, and spice bag. Bring to boiling; cover and simmer 25 minutes. Add oranges. Chill overnight. Remove spice bag before serving. Serves 6.

CEREAL FOR LESS

You pay for convenience with cereals. Reduce what you spend for these foods by considering the following pointers:
● Increase your use of home-cooked cereals. The ready-prepared versions cost more.
● Buy unsweetened cereals in preference to the presweetened versions. Unsweetened cereals are more economical per ounce and may provide better nutrition.
● Compare box sizes to get the best buy for your family. Usually, individual serving packages cost more than larger boxes.

CHICKEN-RICE SCRAPPLE

   2½ cups chicken or turkey broth
    ¼ cup finely chopped celery
     2 tablespoons finely snipped parsley
     1 tablespoon finely chopped onion
     1 cup quick-cooking rice cereal
            ● ● ●
     1 cup ground, cooked or leftover
        chicken, turkey, or ham
        All-purpose flour
        Cooking oil
        Margarine or butter

In saucepan combine broth, celery, parsley, and onion; bring to boiling. Stir in rice cereal. Cook and stir over low heat for 30 seconds. Remove from heat; cover and let stand for 15 minutes. Stir in chicken. Press into a greased 8½x4½x2⅝-inch loaf pan. Chill till firm.
   Unmold and cut into ½-inch slices. Coat slices lightly with flour. In skillet brown slices over low heat in a small amount of hot cooking oil till crisp, 10 to 15 minutes on each side. Serve hot with margarine. Makes 6 servings.

BUTTERSCOTCH OATMEAL

     2 beaten eggs
   3½ cups reconstituted nonfat dry milk
        or fluid milk
     1 cup brown sugar
     2 cups quick-cooking rolled oats
    ¼ cup margarine or butter
        Milk

In large saucepan combine eggs, milk, and sugar. Cook and stir over medium heat till slightly thickened, about 5 minutes. Stir in rolled oats; cook just till mixture begins to bubble, about 3 minutes. (For creamier texture, add oatmeal to *uncooked* egg mixture; cook and stir over medium heat till thickened, 8 to 10 minutes.) Add margarine or butter; cover and remove from heat. Let stand a few minutes, then stir to blend in margarine. Serve with additional milk. Makes 4 to 6 servings.

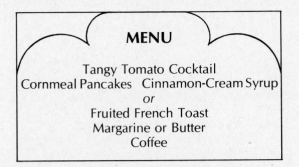

MENU

Tangy Tomato Cocktail
Cornmeal Pancakes   Cinnamon-Cream Syrup
or
Fruited French Toast
Margarine or Butter
Coffee

Greats from the griddle—that's what you'll call these variations of pancakes and French toast. They rate high in taste appeal and in your budget food plan.

TANGY TOMATO COCKTAIL

With white flecks of cottage cheese—

¾ **cup cream-style cottage cheese**
6 **tablespoons reconstituted nonfat
    dry milk or fluid milk**
3 **cups tomato juice, chilled**
1½ **teaspoons Worcestershire sauce**
¾ **teaspoon celery salt**

Place cream-style cottage cheese and milk in blender container. Cover; blend till smooth. Add chilled tomato juice, Worcestershire sauce, and celery salt. Cover; blend till well mixed. Pour into juice glasses. Makes 6 to 8 servings.

CINNAMON-CREAM SYRUP

1 **cup sugar**
½ **cup light corn syrup**
¼ **cup water**
½ **to ¾ teaspoon ground cinnamon**
½ **cup evaporated milk**

In small saucepan combine sugar, corn syrup, water, and cinnamon. Bring to boiling over medium heat, stirring constantly. Cook and stir 2 minutes more. Remove from heat and cool 5 minutes; stir in milk. Serve warm over pancakes. Makes 1⅔ cups.

CORNMEAL PANCAKES

1½ **cups yellow or white cornmeal**
¼ **cup all-purpose flour**
1 **teaspoon baking soda**
1 **teaspoon sugar**
1 **teaspoon salt**
• • •
2 **cups sour milk***
2 **tablespoons cooking oil**
1 **slightly beaten egg yolk**
1 **stiffly beaten egg white**

Stir together cornmeal, flour, baking soda, sugar, and salt. Add sour milk, cooking oil, and beaten egg yolk; blend well. Fold in beaten egg white. Let batter stand for 10 minutes. Bake on hot, lightly greased griddle, turning once. Makes about sixteen 4-inch pancakes.

*Combine 2 tablespoons lemon juice or vinegar with enough sweet milk to make 2 cups; let stand for 5 minutes.

FRUITED FRENCH TOAST

Served with apple syrup—

2½ **cups finely chopped apple**
½ **cup brown sugar**
⅓ **cup water**
2 **teaspoons shredded orange peel
    (optional)**
½ **teaspoon ground cinnamon**
• • •
2 **well-beaten eggs**
⅓ **cup reconstituted nonfat dry milk
    or fluid milk**
⅓ **cup orange juice**
12 **slices white bread
    Shortening**

Combine apple, brown sugar, water, orange peel, and cinnamon. Cook over medium heat till apples are transparent and mixture is the consistency of syrup. Combine eggs, milk, and orange juice. Dip bread into egg mixture. Fry on both sides in small amount of hot shortening till golden brown. Serve hot with apple syrup. Serves 6.

MEALS ON THE DOUBLE

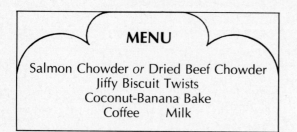

Saving time and saving money often seem to be conflicting goals. However, you can accomplish both by trying this menu and the three menus that follow.

JIFFY BISCUIT TWISTS

1 package refrigerated biscuits (10)
1 tablespoon margarine, melted
2 tablespoons cornmeal
Salt

Cut biscuits in half; roll each to 5-inch stick. Press tops of 2 sticks together; twist together. Seal at bottom. Place on greased baking sheet. Brush with margarine; sprinkle with cornmeal and salt. Bake at 450° for 8 to 10 minutes. Makes 10.

COCONUT-BANANA BAKE

3 firm bananas
2 tablespoons margarine, melted
2 tablespoons light or dark molasses
1 tablespoon lemon juice
2 tablespoons shredded coconut

Peel bananas and cut in half crosswise, then in half lengthwise. Place in a 10x6x 1¾-inch baking dish. Combine next 3 ingredients, 2 tablespoons water, and ¼ teaspoon salt. Pour over bananas; sprinkle with coconut. Bake at 375° for 15 minutes, basting occasionally. Makes 4 servings.

SALMON CHOWDER

1 16-ounce can pink salmon
1 tablespoon finely chopped onion
2 tablespoons margarine or butter
1 10¾-ounce can condensed Cheddar
    cheese soup
¼ cup reconstituted nonfat dry milk
1 16-ounce can tomatoes, cut up
1 tablespoon snipped parsley

Drain salmon, reserving liquid; remove skin and bones, then flake. Cook onion in margarine till tender but not brown. Add soup; gradually blend in reserved salmon liquid and milk. Add undrained tomatoes, salmon, parsley, and dash pepper. Cover and simmer 10 minutes. Serves 4.

DRIED BEEF CHOWDER

⅓ cup chopped onion
2 tablespoons margarine or butter
3 medium potatoes, peeled and diced
1 3-ounce package sliced dried beef,
    snipped (1 cup)
1 16-ounce can cream-style corn
1 cup reconstituted nonfat dry milk
½ teaspoon salt

Cook onion in margarine till tender but not brown. Add potatoes, beef, and 1 cup water; cover and simmer till potatoes are tender, about 15 minutes. Stir in corn and milk. Season with salt and dash pepper; return to boiling. Makes 4 or 5 servings.

Ready in a jiffy

There's nothing costly or complicated about cheesy →
Salmon Chowder. Just simmer together the canned
salmon, onion, Cheddar cheese soup, and canned
tomatoes, then dash with some snipped parsley.

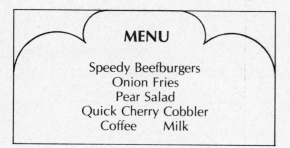

MENU

Speedy Beefburgers
Onion Fries
Pear Salad
Quick Cherry Cobbler
Coffee   Milk

Caught short of time and money? Then, give this family-favored combination, burgers and French fries, a face lift by using recipe variations. They only take minutes to prepare and pennies from your purse.

ONION FRIES

Dip 16 ounces frozen French-fried potatoes (3½ cups) in ¼ cup melted margarine or butter. Place 1 envelope onion soup mix in paper or clear plastic bag. Add potatoes, a few at a time, and shake till coated. Place potatoes in 13x9x2-inch baking pan. Bake at 425° for 15 to 20 minutes, turning once. Makes 6 servings.

QUICK CHERRY COBBLER

1 21-ounce can cherry pie filling
¼ teaspoon almond extract
1 package refrigerated biscuits
    (6 biscuits)
1 tablespoon granulated sugar
1 tablespoon brown sugar
¼ teaspoon ground cinnamon
1 tablespoon margarine, melted
    Whipped dessert topping (optional)

In saucepan combine pie filling and almond extract; bring to boiling. Turn into six 6-ounce custard cups. Top each with a biscuit. Combine granulated sugar, brown sugar, and cinnamon. Brush top of each biscuit with melted margarine; sprinkle with sugar mixture. Bake at 375° for 15 to 20 minutes. Serve with whipped dessert topping, if desired. Makes 6 servings.

SPEEDY BEEFBURGERS

1 egg
½ cup finely crushed saltine crackers
¼ cup catsup
2 teaspoons Worcestershire sauce
½ teaspoon onion powder
¼ teaspoon salt
    Dash pepper
1 pound ground beef
1 tablespoon shortening
1 10¾-ounce can condensed tomato
    soup
1 cup drained whole kernel corn
2 tablespoons reconstituted nonfat
    dry milk or fluid milk
½ teaspoon dried marjoram leaves,
    crushed
    Dash bottled hot pepper
    sauce (optional)

Combine egg, cracker crumbs, catsup, Worcestershire sauce, onion powder, salt, and pepper; add ground beef and mix well. Shape meat mixture into 6 patties. In large skillet brown meat patties on both sides in hot shortening. Combine tomato soup, corn, milk, marjoram, and hot pepper sauce. Pour over meat. Cook, covered, over low heat for 10 minutes. Makes 6 servings.

ECONOMY PLUS CONVENIENCE

Using some convenience foods actually costs you less than if you were to make the same foods from scratch. Some of the biggest convenience food bargains are frozen orange juice concentrate, bottled lemon juice, canned and frozen peas, cake mixes, canned soups, and instant coffee. When time is particularly short, add slightly higher-cost but still economical foods to your convenience purchases: frozen French-fried potatoes, refrigerated biscuits, muffin mixes, and pudding mixes.

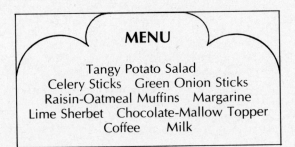

MENU

Tangy Potato Salad
Celery Sticks   Green Onion Sticks
Raisin-Oatmeal Muffins   Margarine
Lime Sherbet   Chocolate-Mallow Topper
Coffee   Milk

The addition of frankfurters turns a salad into main dish fare. To whip it into serving order in double time, cook, peel, dice, and then refrigerate the potatoes a day ahead. Just before serving, simply combine and heat all of the ingredients.

CHOCOLATE-MALLOW TOPPER

**2 1-ounce squares unsweetened
    chocolate**
⅔ cup evaporated milk
**1 10-ounce package miniature
    marshmallows (about 6 cups)**
1 teaspoon vanilla

In saucepan melt chocolate with milk. Add marshmallows; heat till dissolved. Remove from heat; stir in vanilla and dash salt. Serve warm or cool. Makes 2½ cups.

TANGY POTATO SALAD

**1 10½-ounce can condensed cream of
    celery soup**
¼ cup reconstituted nonfat dry milk
2 tablespoons sweet pickle relish
2 tablespoons vinegar
1 tablespoon finely chopped onion
3 cups diced, peeled, cooked potatoes
**8 ounces frankfurters, bias-sliced
    into 1-inch pieces**

In skillet combine first 5 ingredients, ½ teaspoon salt, and dash pepper; cook and stir till boiling. Stir in potatoes and franks; heat through. Top with snipped parsley, if desired. Makes 4 servings.

RAISIN-OATMEAL MUFFINS

1 cup quick-cooking rolled oats
1 cup sour milk*
1 cup sifted all-purpose flour
⅓ cup brown sugar
2 teaspoons baking powder
½ teaspoon baking soda
½ teaspoon salt
1 well-beaten egg
¼ cup cooking oil
½ cup raisins

Mix oats and milk; let stand 15 minutes. Sift dry ingredients. Combine oats, egg, and oil. Make well in dry ingredients; add oats. Stir to moisten; fold in raisins. Fill greased muffin pans ⅔ full. Bake at 425° for 20 minutes. Makes 12.

*Combine 1 tablespoon vinegar with milk to make 1 cup; let stand 5 minutes.

Tangy Potato Salad provides hearty eating and vivid flavor. Chunks of cooked potatoes and frankfurters simmer briefly in a piquant dressing based on cream of celery soup, vinegar, and pickle relish.

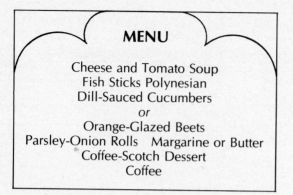

MENU

Cheese and Tomato Soup
Fish Sticks Polynesian
Dill-Sauced Cucumbers
or
Orange-Glazed Beets
Parsley-Onion Rolls   Margarine or Butter
Coffee-Scotch Dessert
Coffee

Low-cost convenience foods — canned soup, frozen fish sticks, refrigerated rolls, and instant pudding — give you a head start on preparing this jiffy meal. For best use of your time, make the casserole first, and while it is baking, fix the rolls, dessert, vegetable, and soup.

COFFEE-SCOTCH DESSERT

    1 4-ounce package instant
        butterscotch pudding mix
    1 teaspoon instant coffee powder
    1 cup vanilla ice cream, softened
    ¼ cup coarse graham cracker crumbs

Prepare pudding mix following package directions; pour into 4 dessert dishes. Chill for short time, if desired. At serving time, stir coffee powder into ice cream; spoon atop pudding. Sprinkle with crumbs. Serve immediately. Makes 4 servings.

PARSLEY-ONION ROLLS

    1 package refrigerated crescent
        rolls (8)
    2 tablespoons margarine, softened
    2 tablespoons snipped parsley
    1 tablespoon instant minced onion

Unroll and separate crescent rolls. Spread with margarine. Sprinkle with parsley and onion. Roll up and bake according to package directions. Makes 8 rolls.

FISH STICKS POLYNESIAN

A good use for leftover rice —

    ⅓ cup sugar
    2 tablespoons cornstarch
    1 13¾-ounce can pineapple tidbits
    2 teaspoons soy sauce
    1 vegetable bouillon cube
    ¼ teaspoon salt
    2 tablespoons vinegar
 1½ cups cooked or leftover rice
    1 10-ounce package frozen peas,
        thawed
    1 8-ounce package frozen, fried,
        breaded fish sticks
    Carrot curls

In medium saucepan combine sugar and cornstarch. Drain pineapple tidbits, reserving ⅔ cup syrup. Gradually stir reserved syrup into sugar mixture. Add soy sauce, vegetable bouillon cube, and salt. Cook, stirring constantly, till thickened and bubbly. Remove from heat; stir in vinegar. Combine cooked rice, thawed peas, and pineapple tidbits. Stir sauce into rice mixture; turn into 1-quart casserole.

Arrange fish spoke-fashion atop rice mixture. Bake at 350° for 25 to 30 minutes. Top with carrot curls. Serves 4.

CHEESE AND TOMATO SOUP

A canned soup fix-up —

    1 10¾-ounce can condensed tomato
        soup
    ⅔ cup evaporated milk
    ⅔ cup water
    4 ounces process cheese spread,
        shredded (1 cup)
    ½ teaspoon Worcestershire sauce
    Dash garlic powder

In saucepan blend tomato soup with evaporated milk and water; add shredded process cheese spread, Worcestershire sauce, and garlic powder. Heat and stir mixture till cheese melts. Makes 4 servings.

You needn't get befuddled when unexpected company arrives. Using foods that you have on hand, serve a three-course dinner in no time at all. Feature delicious Fish Sticks Polynesian as the main course.

DILL-SAUCED CUCUMBERS

1 chicken bouillon cube
½ cup boiling water
1 tablespoon margarine or butter
1 tablespoon all-purpose flour
½ teaspoon sugar
½ teaspoon dillweed
¼ teaspoon salt
¼ cup reconstituted nonfat dry milk
2 teaspoons vinegar
2 unpeeled cucumbers, sliced

Dissolve bouillon cube in boiling water. In saucepan melt margarine. Stir in flour, sugar, dillweed, and salt. Add bouillon, milk, and vinegar; heat and stir till thickened and bubbly. Add cucumbers; cook, covered, over low heat for 10 to 15 minutes, stirring occasionally. Serves 4.

ORANGE-GLAZED BEETS

Subtle caraway flavor—

1 16-ounce can beets
1 tablespoon sugar
1 tablespoon cornstarch
¼ teaspoon caraway seed
¼ teaspoon salt
• • •
¼ cup orange juice
2 tablespoons margarine or butter

Drain beets, reserving ⅓ cup liquid. In saucepan combine sugar, cornstarch, caraway seed, and salt. Stir in reserved beet liquid, orange juice, and margarine or butter. Cook, stirring constantly, till mixture is thickened and clear. Add beets; heat through. Makes 4 servings.

MONEY-SAVING MAIN DISHES

Did you know that the main dish is the best place to start cutting food costs? It's true, for meat purchases take the biggest chunk (about one-third) out of your food dollar.

This section of tempting recipes will help you to cut main dish costs three ways. First, prepare low-cost protein foods like the Hearty Cost-Cutters. It's easy to fit these beef, pork, variety meat, poultry, fish, cheese, and egg dishes into your menus. Second, serve some of the Satisfying Budget-Stretchers. These tantalizing casseroles, stews, soups, salads, and sandwiches include economical extenders such as pasta and rice, which make the meat or other protein food go further. Third, develop flavorful main dishes with leftovers, using the leftover chart and recipe ideas at the end of the section as a guide.

For a budget version of an Italian favorite, serve Mock Lasagne Casserole made with ground beef, cottage and process cheeses, and elbow macaroni.

HEARTY COST-CUTTERS

SWEET-SOUR BEEF STEW

1½ pounds beef stew meat, cut in
    1-inch cubes
2 tablespoons cooking oil
1 cup chopped carrot
1 cup sliced onion
1 8-ounce can tomato sauce (1 cup)
¼ cup brown sugar
¼ cup vinegar
1 tablespoon Worcestershire sauce
4 teaspoons cornstarch
    Hot cooked noodles
    Poppy seed (optional)

Brown meat in hot oil. Add next 6 ingredients, ½ cup water, and 1 teaspoon salt. Cover and cook over low heat till meat is tender, about 2 hours. Combine cornstarch and ¼ cup cold water; add to beef mixture. Cook and stir till thickened and bubbly. Serve over noodles sprinkled with poppy seed. Garnish with carrot curls and parsley, if desired. Makes 4 servings.

PIONEER STEW

Cook 1 pound ground beef, ½ cup chopped onion, and ½ cup chopped green pepper till meat is browned and vegetables are tender. Drain off fat. Drain and reserve liquids from one 16-ounce can whole kernel corn, one 16-ounce can tomatoes, and one 15-ounce can red kidney beans. Add reserved liquid, 1 teaspoon chili powder, and ¾ teaspoon salt to meat mixture. Simmer, uncovered, till liquid is reduced to half, 20 minutes; stir occasionally.

Add corn, tomatoes, and beans; simmer 10 minutes, stirring occasionally. Combine 1 tablespoon all-purpose flour and 2 tablespoons water. Stir into stew. Cook and stir till thickened and bubbly. Stir in 2 ounces sharp process American cheese, shredded (½ cup), till melted. Serves 6.

SHAKER HERB-BEEF STEW

1 pound beef stew meat, cut in
    1-inch cubes
1 tablespoon all-purpose flour
1 teaspoon salt
    Dash pepper
1 tablespoon cooking oil
1 medium onion, sliced
½ cup apple juice or cider
1 medium rutabaga, peeled and
    diced (about 2 cups)
3 large carrots, peeled and
    diced (about 1 cup)
1 tablespoon snipped parsley
¾ teaspoon salt
⅛ teaspoon dried marjoram leaves,
    crushed
⅛ teaspoon dried thyme leaves,
    crushed
2 tablespoons all-purpose flour
4 to 5 servings hot mashed potatoes

Coat beef cubes with mixture of 1 tablespoon flour, 1 teaspoon salt, and pepper. In 3-quart saucepan brown beef cubes in hot oil; add onion, apple juice, and 1 cup water. Cover; simmer over low heat till meat is tender, 1½ hours. Add rutabaga, carrots, 1 cup water, parsley, the ¾ teaspoon salt, marjoram, and thyme. Simmer, covered, till vegetables are tender, 30 minutes. Blend ¼ cup water and the 2 tablespoons flour; add to stew mixture. Cook and stir till mixture is thickened and bubbly. Pour stew into serving dish. Spoon potatoes around edge. Serves 4 or 5.

Beef-lover's special

Chopped carrot, tomato sauce, brown sugar, and →
vinegar give Sweet-Sour Beef Stew its distinctive taste. Nestle the meat in a bed of poppy seed noodles, then decorate it with parsley and carrot curls.

BRAISED SHORT RIBS

　3 pounds beef short ribs, cut in
　　serving-sized pieces
　¾ cup uncooked long-grain rice
　½ cup chopped onion
　½ cup chopped celery
　¼ cup chopped green pepper
　1 teaspoon Worcestershire sauce
　¼ teaspoon dried thyme leaves,
　　crushed

In skillet brown ribs slowly. Season with salt. Place in 3-quart casserole. Cover; bake at 325° for 1 hour. In same skillet combine rice, onion, celery, and green pepper; cook till rice is lightly browned. After meat has baked, remove ribs from casserole; pour off fat. Place rice mixture in casserole; top with ribs. Combine 2¼ cups water, 2 teaspoons salt, Worcestershire, thyme, and ⅛ teaspoon pepper; heat to boiling. Pour over ribs. Cover; bake 1 hour more. Serves 4 to 6.

GOULASH

　2 pounds beef chuck, cubed
　2 tablespoons shortening
　1 cup chopped onion
　1 8-ounce can tomato sauce (1 cup)
　1 tablespoon sugar
　1 tablespoon paprika
　2 tablespoons vinegar
　2 teaspoons Worcestershire sauce
　⅛ teaspoon garlic powder
　2 bay leaves
　　　• • •
　2 tablespoons all-purpose flour
　　Hot cooked noodles

In large saucepan brown beef in hot short-ening. Add next 8 ingredients, 1 cup water, 1 teaspoon salt, and ⅛ teaspoon pepper. Cover and simmer, stirring occasionally, till tender, 1½ to 2 hours. Remove bay leaves. Skim off excess fat. Blend flour with ¼ cup cold water; stir into meat mix-ture. Cook and stir till thickened and bubbly. Cook and stir 1 minute longer. Serve over noodles. Serves 5 or 6.

TRIM MEAT COSTS

Use the hints below and information on pages 90-92 to help you save on meats:
● Since fat and bone are often included in the meat you buy, use cost per serving as the buying guide rather than price per pound. You may often save by paying more per pound for lean, boneless meat.
● Stick to average-sized meat servings (2 to 3 ounces cooked, lean meat). To satisfy heartier eaters, serve more of the less-expensive foods such as breads.

STUFFED BEEF ROLLS

　¼ cup chopped onion
　¼ cup chopped green pepper
　2 tablespoons margarine or butter
　1 cup cooked or leftover rice
　¼ teaspoon dried oregano leaves,
　　crushed
　1½ pounds beef round steak, cut
　　¼ inch thick
　2 tablespoons all-purpose flour
　2 tablespoons shortening
　1 8-ounce can tomato sauce (1 cup)
　1 tablespoon brown sugar
　2 teaspoons Worcestershire sauce
　1 beef bouillon cube, crushed

Cook onion and green pepper in margarine till tender. Remove from heat; combine onion mixture with rice and oregano. Cut steak into 6 rectangular pieces; pound *each* to a 6x4-inch rectangle. Place about 2 tablespoons rice mixture on *each* steak; roll up jelly-roll fashion, tucking in edges. Tie or skewer securely.

　Coat meat rolls with mixture of flour, 1 teaspoon salt, and dash pepper. Brown meat slowly in hot shortening. Combine remaining ingredients and ¾ cup water; pour over meat. Cover and simmer 1 hour. Remove cord or skewers. Serves 6.

SIMMERED BEEF SHANKS

    2 **tablespoons all-purpose flour**
    3 **to 4 pounds cross-cut beef shanks**
    1 **tablespoon cooking oil**
    1 **cup tomato juice**
    2 **tablespoons snipped parsley**
    ½ **teaspoon dried basil leaves,
        crushed**
    4 **medium potatoes, peeled and
        quartered**
    2 **tablespoons all-purpose flour**

Combine 2 tablespoons flour, 1 tablespoon salt, and ¼ teaspoon pepper in paper or plastic bag. Add shanks, one at a time; shake to coat. In Dutch oven brown meat in hot oil. Add tomato juice, parsley, and basil. Cover; simmer 1½ hours. Add potatoes; cover and simmer till tender, 30 to 45 minutes more. Remove meat and potatoes.

    Skim excess fat from pan juices. Add enough water to juices to make 1 cup liquid; return to pan. Combine ½ cup water and the 2 tablespoons all-purpose flour; stir into juices. Cook and stir till thickened and bubbly. Serves 4 to 6.

SAUCY MEATBALLS

    1 **slightly beaten egg**
    1 **cup soft bread crumbs**
    ¼ **cup reconstituted nonfat dry milk**
    ¼ **teaspoon dried oregano leaves,
        crushed**
    ⅛ **teaspoon dried thyme leaves,
        crushed**
    Dash pepper
    1½ **pounds ground beef**
    2 **tablespoons shortening**
    1 **10½-ounce can condensed cream of
        mushroom soup**
    Hot cooked rice or noodles

Mix first 6 ingredients; mix in meat. Shape into 30 balls; brown in hot fat. Drain off fat. Blend soup and ⅔ cup water; pour over meat. Simmer, uncovered, for 20 to 25 minutes, stirring occasionally. Serve with rice or noodles. Makes 6 servings.

SAVORY POT ROAST

    1 **3-pound beef chuck roast**
    ⅓ **cup grape jelly**
    3 **medium onions, sliced**
    ⅓ **cup vinegar**
    1 **teaspoon Kitchen Bouquet (optional)**
    ½ **teaspoon ground ginger**
    2 **bay leaves**
    ¼ **cup all-purpose flour**

Trim excess fat from the meat; heat trimmings in Dutch oven till 2 tablespoons fat accumulate. Discard trimmings. Slowly brown meat in hot fat. Remove from heat. Season with 2 teaspoons salt and ¼ teaspoon pepper. Spread jelly over meat; top with onion. Combine vinegar, ¼ cup water, Kitchen Bouquet, ginger, and bay leaves; pour over meat. Cover and cook 2 to 2½ hours, adding water if needed.

    Remove meat to warm platter; discard bay leaves. Pour pan juices into large measuring cup; skim fat, reserving ¼ cup. Add water to juices to make 2 cups. Return fat to pan; stir in flour. Add juices. Cook and stir till thickened and bubbly; cook and stir 3 to 4 minutes. Season with salt and pepper. Makes 8 servings.

VEGETABLE POT ROAST

Bring 1 cup dry lima beans and 3 cups water to boil; simmer about 2 minutes. Remove from heat. Let stand 1 hour. Do not drain. Trim fat from one 3-pound beef chuck roast. In Dutch oven heat trimmings till 2 tablespoons fat accumulate; discard the trimmings. Brown the meat in hot fat. Remove the meat; drain off excess fat.

    Combine undrained beans, 1 cup chopped onion, ½ cup catsup, 1 teaspoon salt, ⅛ teaspoon garlic powder, and ⅛ teaspoon pepper in Dutch oven. Top with meat. Simmer, covered, 2 hours. Add 5 medium carrots, sliced; cook 30 minutes more. Remove meat to warm platter. Combine 1 tablespoon all-purpose flour and 2 tablespoons water; stir into vegetable mixture. Cook and stir till bubbly. Serves 8.

OLD-FASHIONED POT ROAST

1 4-pound beef chuck roast
2 tablespoons all-purpose flour
2 teaspoons salt
½ teaspoon dried marjoram leaves, crushed
¼ teaspoon dried thyme leaves, crushed
¼ teaspoon dried basil leaves, crushed
¼ teaspoon pepper
½ onion, sliced
3 medium onions, cut in sixths
1 pound carrots, peeled and cut up
1 pound small potatoes, peeled
½ teaspoon salt
¼ cup all-purpose flour
　Snipped parsley

Trim excess fat from meat. In Dutch oven heat trimmings till 1 tablespoon fat accumulates; discard trimmings. Rub meat with 2 tablespoons flour. Brown the meat in hot fat. Season with salt, marjoram, thyme, basil, and pepper. Add sliced onion and 1 cup water. Cover; cook at 350° for 2 hours. Add vegetables and ½ cup water; sprinkle with ½ teaspoon salt. Cover; cook till meat and vegetables are tender, 1 to 1½ hours. Remove to warm platter.

Skim fat from juices. Add water to juices to make 1½ cups. Combine ½ cup cold water and ¼ cup flour; shake. Stir into juices; cook and stir till thickened and bubbly. Season with salt and pepper. Simmer 2 to 3 minutes, stirring occasionally. Pour some gravy over meat. Top with parsley. Pass extra gravy. Serves 6 to 8.

Old-Fashioned Pot Roast with all its trimmings is the classic budget-balancing meal. Placed beside the beef are cooked-to-perfection potatoes, carrots, and onions, all draped with a rich, brown gravy.

BARBECUED HAM ROAST

Basted with a zesty sauce —

> 1 3- to 4-pound fully cooked ham
>   (butt portion)
> ½ cup catsup
> ⅓ cup chopped onion
> ¼ cup vinegar
> ¼ cup light or dark molasses
> 1 teaspoon Worcestershire sauce
> 1 teaspoon prepared mustard
> ½ teaspoon chili powder

Place ham on rack in shallow roasting pan. Roast at 325° till meat thermometer registers 130°, about 1½ hours. Meanwhile, in small saucepan combine catsup, chopped onion, vinegar, molasses, Worcestershire sauce, mustard, and chili powder. Simmer, stirring occasionally, till onion is tender, about 15 minutes. During the last 30 minutes of roasting, spoon barbecue sauce over ham several times. Pass remaining sauce with meat. Serves 9 to 12.

GLAZED PORK SHOULDER

Delicately spiced with ginger —

> 1 4- to 5-pound fresh pork
>   shoulder roast
> 6 to 8 medium sweet potatoes
> 1 8¾-ounce can crushed pineapple,
>   drained
> ½ cup dark or light corn syrup
> 2 teaspoons prepared mustard
> ½ teaspoon ground ginger

Place meat on rack in shallow roasting pan. Roast at 325° till meat thermometer registers 170°, about 3 to 3¾ hours. Meanwhile, cook potatoes in boiling, salted water till tender; drain and cool. Peel potatoes; halve lengthwise. Combine remaining ingredients. When meat thermometer reaches 170°, remove from oven; arrange potatoes around roast. Spoon glaze over roast and potatoes. Return to oven; roast 20 minutes more. Serves 12 to 15.

SMOKED PORK DINNER

> 1 3- to 4-pound cook-before-eating
>   smoked picnic shoulder
> 1 medium onion, chopped (½ cup)
> ½ cup chopped celery
> ¼ teaspoon garlic powder
> 1 bay leaf
> 6 medium potatoes, peeled and halved
> 6 medium carrots, peeled and halved
> 2 10-ounce packages frozen Brussels
>   sprouts

Place meat in Dutch oven; cover with water. Add onion, celery, garlic powder, and bay leaf. Cover; bring to boiling. Reduce heat; simmer till almost tender, 2½ to 3 hours. Add potatoes and carrots; cover and simmer for about 15 minutes. Add Brussels sprouts; simmer 15 to 20 minutes. Discard the bay leaf. Makes 9 to 12 servings.

PORK CHOP DINNER

> 3 cups uncooked noodles
> 1 16-ounce can tomatoes
> 1 teaspoon salt
> 6 pork rib chops, cut ½ inch thick
> ½ cup chopped onion
> 1 beef bouillon cube
> ½ teaspoon dried thyme leaves,
>   crushed
> Dash pepper

Cook noodles in boiling, salted water just till tender; drain. Drain tomatoes, reserving ¾ cup juice. Quarter tomatoes; stir into noodles along with ½ *teaspoon* salt. Place noodles in an 11¾x7½x1¾-inch baking dish. Trim fat from chops. In skillet cook trimmings till 2 tablespoons fat accumulate; discard trimmings. Brown the chops in hot fat. Arrange chops over noodles. Sprinkle with onion.

In small saucepan combine reserved tomato juice, bouillon cube, remaining salt, thyme, and pepper. Cook and stir till bouillon cube is dissolved; pour over chops. Cover; bake at 350° till meat is tender, about 1¼ hours. Makes 6 servings.

DRESSED-UP PORK STEAKS

4 pork blade or arm steaks
(about 2 pounds)
1 egg
2½ cups soft bread crumbs
½ cup finely chopped celery
¼ cup finely chopped onion
1 teaspoon grated orange peel
(optional)
½ cup orange juice
½ teaspoon ground sage

Trim excess fat from steaks. In skillet heat trimmings till 2 tablespoons fat accumulate; discard trimmings. Brown steaks on both sides in hot fat; pour off excess fat. Season steaks with salt and pepper.

Beat egg. Add remaining ingredients and ¼ teaspoon salt; toss together lightly. Mound dressing atop steaks. Place steaks in skillet; pour ½ cup water over. Cover; simmer for 30 minutes. Uncover; simmer 5 minutes longer. Makes 4 servings.

ORANGE PORK STEAKS

6 blade or arm bone pork steaks
(about 2½ pounds)
4 medium sweet potatoes, peeled and
cut in ½-inch-thick slices
2 medium oranges
½ cup brown sugar
Dash ground cinnamon
Dash ground nutmeg

Trim excess fat from steaks. In skillet cook trimmings till 1 tablespoon fat accumulates; discard trimmings. Cook steaks slowly just till browned; sprinkle with salt. In a 13½x-8¾x1¾-inch baking dish arrange sweet potatoes. Slice one of the oranges thinly; place atop potatoes. Cover with steaks. Squeeze remaining orange; add water to juice to measure ½ cup. Combine orange juice, brown sugar, ⅛ teaspoon salt, and spices. Pour over steaks. Bake, covered, at 350° for 45 minutes. Uncover; bake 30 minutes more. Garnish with parsley, if desired. Makes 6 servings.

PORK CHOP BUDGET-BALANCERS

Rib, blade, arm, and loin end pork chops are just as nutritious and good tasting as center-cut chops, but usually cost less.

PORK AND POTATO SUPPER

6 pork blade or arm steaks
(about 2½ pounds)
¼ cup all-purpose flour
1 teaspoon salt
Dash pepper
1 10½-ounce can condensed chicken
broth
4 medium potatoes, peeled and sliced
½ inch thick (4 cups)
2 medium onions, thinly sliced
2 tablespoons snipped parsley
Paprika

Trim the excess fat from pork steaks. In a large skillet heat the trimmings till about 2 tablespoons fat accumulate; discard the trimmings. Combine flour, 1 teaspoon salt, and dash pepper; coat meat with flour mixture. In skillet brown steaks on both sides in hot fat, about 10 to 15 minutes. Drain off any excess fat.

Add broth. Cover tightly and simmer till almost tender, about 25 to 30 minutes. Place potato and onion slices over meat; season with salt and pepper. Cover and simmer till potatoes are tender, about 25 to 30 minutes longer. Sprinkle with parsley and paprika. Makes 6 servings.

Well-seasoned meat

*Orange Pork Steaks with sweet potatoes feature →
fresh citrus flavor and just a hint of spices. Drizzle
the extra pan juices over each serving. Prepare
crumb-topped, chopped broccoli for a side dish.*

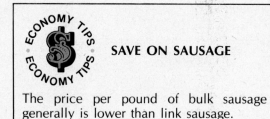

HOCKS AND BEANS

    4 large smoked ham hocks
    1 28-ounce can pork and beans in
        tomato sauce
    1 large unpeeled apple, diced
    1 medium onion, chopped
    ¼ cup catsup
    ¼ cup light or dark molasses
    2 teaspoons prepared horseradish

Place hocks in Dutch oven. Combine remaining ingredients. Pour over hocks. Bake, uncovered, at 325° till tender, about 2 hours; stir occasionally. Serves 6.

FRANK AND CABBAGE ROLLS

Immerse 8 to 10 large cabbage leaves (heavy center vein of leaf may be cut out about 2 inches) in boiling water just till limp, 3 minutes; drain. Combine 1½ cups cooked or leftover rice; 2 ounces process American cheese, shredded (½ cup); ¼ cup chopped onion; ¼ cup reconstituted nonfat dry milk or fluid milk; ½ teaspoon paprika; and ¼ teaspoon salt. Mix thoroughly.

Cut ½ pound frankfurters in half crosswise. Place 3 to 4 tablespoons rice mixture in center of each cabbage leaf; top with frank half. Fold in sides of each leaf and roll ends over meat-rice mixture; fasten with a wooden pick.

In skillet combine one 8-ounce can tomato sauce (1 cup), ½ cup water, 1 tablespoon brown sugar, 1 tablespoon prepared mustard, and ½ teaspoon chili powder. Place cabbage rolls in sauce. Cover; simmer 30 minutes, basting often. Serves 4 or 5.

SAUSAGE BAKE

    1 pound bulk pork sausage
    2 tablespoons sugar
    1 tablespoon all-purpose flour
    ¼ teaspoon ground cinnamon
    2 medium sweet potatoes, peeled and
        sliced
    3 medium apples, peeled and sliced

Brown sausage, breaking up large pieces. Drain off fat. Blend sugar, flour, cinnamon, ¼ teaspoon salt, and ½ cup cold water. Combine all ingredients in 2-quart casserole; cover. Bake at 375° till potatoes and apples are tender, about 45 minutes; stir once or twice. Serves 4 to 6.

LAMB SHANKS WITH BEANS

    1 cup dry pinto beans
    4 lamb shanks
    2 tablespoons cooking oil
    ½ cup chopped onion
    1 cup chicken broth
    ½ teaspoon salt
    ½ teaspoon dried oregano leaves,
        crushed
    1 bay leaf
    2 cups sliced carrots
    2 tablespoons all-purpose flour

In saucepan combine beans and 2½ cups cold water. Bring to boiling; simmer 2 minutes. Remove from heat. Let stand 1 hour. Do not drain. In large skillet slowly brown shanks in hot oil for 25 to 30 minutes; remove from pan. Drain off excess fat.

To skillet add beans with liquid, onion, broth, salt, oregano, dash pepper, and bay leaf. Place shanks on top. Bring to boiling. Reduce heat; simmer, covered, for about 1 hour. Add the sliced carrots; simmer, covered, 30 to 45 minutes more. Remove the shanks to serving platter; discard bay leaf. Skim fat from bean mixture. Blend the flour with ¼ cup cold water; stir into bean mixture. Cook and stir till thickened and bubbly. Cook and stir 1 to 2 minutes more. Makes 4 servings.

BARBECUED TONGUE

1 2-pound beef tongue
4 bay leaves
2 tablespoons vinegar
¼ cup chopped celery
¼ cup chopped green pepper
2 tablespoons margarine or butter
1 10¾-ounce can condensed tomato
  soup
2 tablespoons brown sugar
3 tablespoons vinegar
1 tablespoon Worcestershire sauce
1½ teaspoons prepared horseradish
1 teaspoon chili powder
  Hot cooked rice

Place tongue in Dutch oven. Cover with water; add 1 teaspoon salt, ½ teaspoon pepper, bay leaves, and 2 tablespoons vinegar. Cover; simmer till tender, 2 hours. Plunge into cold water. When cool enough to handle, remove from water. Cut off gristle. Make lengthwise slit on underside. Peel off skin. Chill tongue. Cut meat in thin, crosswise slices; cut in strips.

Cook celery and green pepper in margarine till tender but not brown. Blend in ¼ cup water and remaining ingredients *except* rice. Add tongue; stir to coat. Simmer, uncovered, for 20 minutes, stirring occasionally. Serve over rice. Serves 8.

SWEET-SOUR LIVER

Cut 1 pound beef liver into 2x½-inch strips; brown in 2 tablespoons hot shortening. Stir in 1 cup water, 1 beef bouillon cube, and ¼ teaspoon salt. Cover and simmer over low heat for 5 minutes. Drain one 13½-ounce can pineapple tidbits, reserving syrup. In saucepan combine 3 tablespoons brown sugar, 2 tablespoons cornstarch, and ¼ teaspoon salt. Add reserved syrup, 2 to 3 tablespoons vinegar, and 1 tablespoon soy sauce. Cook and stir till thickened.

Add sauce to liver; mix well. Stir in pineapple and 1 medium green pepper, cut in strips; cook and stir 5 minutes. Serve over hot cooked rice. Makes 4 servings.

KIDNEY-VEGETABLE PIE

1 beef kidney
1 pound beef stew meat, cut in
  ½-inch cubes
¼ cup all-purpose flour
2 tablespoons shortening
1½ cups tomato juice
1 medium onion, sliced
¼ teaspoon dried thyme leaves,
  crushed
3 medium carrots, sliced
3 stalks celery, sliced
1 10-ounce package frozen lima beans
  or one 16-ounce can green lima
  beans, drained
1 tablespoon all-purpose flour
  Pastry Topper

Remove membrane and hard parts from kidney. In saucepan combine kidney, 4 cups water, and 1 tablespoon salt. Soak for 1 hour; drain. Cover with cold water. Bring to boiling; simmer, covered, 20 minutes. Drain; cut kidney in ½-inch cubes.

Coat stew meat with ¼ cup flour. In Dutch oven brown stew meat in hot shortening. Add tomato juice, 1 cup water, onion, 1¼ teaspoons salt, and thyme; cover and simmer till meat is almost tender, about 1 hour. Stir in carrots, celery, and limas; simmer, covered, till vegetables are tender, 30 minutes. Add kidney; bring mixture to boiling. Combine 2 tablespoons cold water and 1 tablespoon flour; stir into stew. Cook and stir till thickened and bubbly. Pour into 2-quart casserole. Place Pastry Topper atop *hot* mixture. Bake at 450° till pastry is lightly browned, about 15 to 20 minutes. Serves 6.

Pastry Topper: Sift together 1½ cups sifted all-purpose flour and ½ teaspoon salt. Cut in ½ cup shortening till pieces are the size of small peas. Sprinkle 1 tablespoon cold water over part of mixture; gently toss with fork. Repeat with additional 3 to 4 tablespoons cold water till all mixture is moistened. Form into ball. Roll out on lightly floured surface to 8-inch circle, ¼ inch thick. Cut pastry in 6 pie-shaped wedges; prick with fork.

FRUITED ROAST TURKEY

2 cups chopped celery
½ cup chopped onion
6 tablespoons margarine or butter
7 cups ½-inch dry bread cubes
1½ cups chopped apple
1 beaten egg
1½ teaspoons poultry seasoning
1 6-ounce can frozen orange juice
    concentrate, thawed
1 10-pound ready-to-cook turkey
1 16-ounce can whole cranberry sauce
½ cup light corn syrup

Cook celery and onion in 4 *tablespoons* margarine till tender. Add next 4 ingredients, 1 teaspoon salt, and ⅛ teaspoon pepper; mix. Stir in ⅓ cup juice concentrate.

Rinse turkey; pat dry. Stuff wishbone cavity lightly; skewer neck skin to back. Sprinkle large cavity with salt. Spoon in stuffing. Slip legs under band of skin across opening or tie to tail. Cover turkey loosely with foil. Roast at 325° for 4 to 4½ hours. Meanwhile, in saucepan combine cranberry sauce, syrup, and remaining margarine and juice concentrate. Heat through, stirring occasionally.

Cut band of skin or string between legs and tail. Uncover and spoon cranberry glaze over. Continue roasting till done, 30 minutes more; brush occasionally with glaze. Place turkey on platter. Garnish with parsley, orange slices, and cranberries, if desired. Pass remaining glaze.

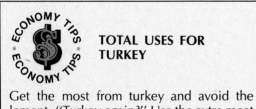

TOTAL USES FOR TURKEY

Get the most from turkey and avoid the lament, "Turkey again?" Use the extra meat in a variety of casseroles, salads, sandwiches, and skillet meals. And when there's a little meat clinging to the bones, make a tasty soup (see page 62).

TURKEY-VEGETABLE BAKE

2 tablespoons margarine or butter
2 tablespoons all-purpose flour
1 cup turkey broth or 1 chicken
    bouillon cube dissolved in 1 cup
    boiling water
2 cups diced, cooked or leftover
    turkey
1 10-ounce package frozen mixed
    vegetables, cooked and drained,
    or 1 16-ounce can mixed vege-
    tables, drained
3 ounces sharp process American
    cheese, shredded (¾ cup)
½ cup soft bread crumbs

Melt margarine; blend in flour. Add broth; cook and stir till thickened and bubbly. Remove from heat; stir in turkey, vegetables, and ½ cup of the cheese. Turn into a 1-quart casserole. Combine crumbs and remaining cheese; sprinkle over casserole. Bake at 350° till heated through, 30 to 35 minutes. Makes 4 or 5 servings.

TURKEY CREOLE

Cook ½ cup chopped green pepper, ½ cup chopped celery, and ¼ cup chopped onion in 1 tablespoon margarine till tender. Blend in 1 tablespoon all-purpose flour.

Add one 16-ounce can tomatoes, cut up; one 8-ounce can tomato sauce; 1 teaspoon sugar; ½ teaspoon salt; ¼ teaspoon garlic powder; 1 bay leaf; dash pepper; and dash bottled hot pepper sauce (optional). Cook and stir till thickened and bubbly. Add 1½ cups diced, cooked or leftover turkey. Cover; simmer for 5 to 10 minutes. Serve over hot cooked rice. Makes 6 servings.

Spectacular turkey

Fruited Roast Turkey is worthy of many repeat performances. The flavor-filled stuffing contains apples and orange juice. Baste the bird with cranberry glaze to give it the picture-pretty gloss.

TURKEY-POTATO PANCAKES

An excellent use for leftover turkey —

> 3 beaten eggs
> 3 cups shredded, raw potato,
>   drained (about 3 potatoes)
> 1½ cups finely chopped, cooked or
>   leftover turkey
> 1½ teaspoons grated onion
>   Dash pepper
> 1 tablespoon all-purpose flour
> 1½ teaspoons salt
>   Canned cranberry sauce

In mixing bowl combine eggs, potato, turkey, onion, and pepper. Add flour and salt; mix well. Using about ¼ cup batter for each pancake, drop batter onto hot, greased griddle, spreading to about 4 inches in diameter. Cook over medium-low heat for 3 to 4 minutes on each side. Serve with cranberry sauce. Makes 15 pancakes.

OVEN CHICKEN FRICASSEE

Rice is the perfect accompaniment —

> 3 tablespoons all-purpose flour
> 1 teaspoon salt
> 1 teaspoon paprika
> 1 2½- to 3-pound ready-to-cook
>   broiler-fryer chicken, cut up
> 2 tablespoons margarine or butter,
>   melted
> 1 10½-ounce can condensed cream of
>   mushroom soup
> ⅔ cup evaporated milk

Combine flour, salt, and paprika. Brush chicken with melted margarine; coat with flour mixture. Arrange chicken in an 11¾x-7½x1¾-inch baking dish. Bake at 375° for 20 minutes. Drain off excess fat.

   Meanwhile, in saucepan combine soup and milk; cook and stir till heated through. Pour mixture over chicken. Cover baking dish with foil. Continue baking till chicken is tender, about 40 minutes. Remove foil the last 10 minutes. Serves 4.

PERK UP FOODS INEXPENSIVELY

The appearance of a food contributes greatly to its eye- and taste-appeal. Often, a pretty serving dish and a little time spent arranging the food attractively is all that's needed. Other times, using one of the following simple and inexpensive garnishes adds a great deal of interest: parsley, onion rings, carrot curls, paprika, orange or lemon wedges or slices, radish roses, grated or shredded cheese, croutons, hard-cooked egg slices, sieved egg yolk, apple wedges or rings, lettuce or cabbage leaves.

CHICKEN SKILLET

> ⅓ cup sifted all-purpose flour
> 1 teaspoon salt
> 1 teaspoon paprika
> ¼ teaspoon ground sage
> 1 2½- to 3-pound ready-to-cook
>   broiler-fryer chicken, cut up
> ¼ cup shortening
> 1 teaspoon sugar
> 1 13¾-ounce can chicken broth
> 1 tablespoon lemon juice
> 1 cup sliced carrots
> 1 medium onion, sliced
> 2 tablespoons snipped parsley

Combine flour, salt, paprika, sage, and ¼ teaspoon pepper in paper or plastic bag; add chicken, a few pieces at a time, and shake. Reserve excess flour mixture. In skillet brown chicken on all sides in hot shortening. Remove chicken from skillet. Stir reserved flour mixture and sugar into pan drippings; add chicken broth. Cook and stir till thickened and bubbly. Stir in lemon juice, carrots, onion, and parsley. Arrange chicken atop vegetable mixture. Cover and cook till vegetables and chicken are tender, 40 to 45 minutes; stir occasionally. Makes 4 servings.

CHICKEN WITH ORANGE

  1 2½- to 3-pound ready-to-cook
     broiler-fryer chicken, cut up
  2 tablespoons shortening
  ½ teaspoon paprika
  1 medium onion, sliced
  ½ 6-ounce can frozen orange juice
     concentrate, thawed (⅓ cup)
  2 tablespoons brown sugar
  2 tablespoons snipped parsley
  2 teaspoons soy sauce
  ½ teaspoon ground ginger
    Hot cooked rice

In skillet brown chicken on all sides in hot shortening; sprinkle with 1 teaspoon salt and paprika. Arrange onion over chicken. Combine juice concentrate, brown sugar, parsley, soy, ginger, and ⅓ cup water; pour over chicken and onion. Cover; simmer till chicken is tender, 35 to 40 minutes. Serve over rice. Makes 4 servings.

SPANISH CHICKEN

  ⅓ cup all-purpose flour
  ½ teaspoon garlic powder
  1 2½- to 3-pound ready-to-cook
     broiler-fryer chicken, cut up
  ¼ cup shortening
  ⅔ cup uncooked long-grain rice
  1 28-ounce can tomatoes
  1 16-ounce can garbanzo beans,
     drained
  1 8-ounce can tomato sauce (1 cup)
  1 teaspoon sugar
  1 teaspoon chili powder

Combine flour, 1 teaspoon salt, and garlic powder in paper or plastic bag; add chicken, a few pieces at a time and shake. In large skillet brown chicken on all sides in hot shortening; remove chicken. In skillet combine remaining ingredients and ¾ teaspoon salt; bring to boiling. Top with browned chicken pieces; reduce heat and cover. Simmer till chicken and rice are tender, 40 to 45 minutes; stir occasionally. Makes 4 servings.

RICE-STUFFED CHICKEN

Pictured on contents page —

  ½ cup chopped celery
  ½ cup chopped onion
  ⅓ cup chopped green pepper
  2 tablespoons margarine or butter
  2 chicken livers
  1½ cups cooked or leftover rice
  1 16-ounce can tomatoes, cut up
  ½ teaspoon rubbed or ground sage
  2 3-pound ready-to-cook roasting
     chickens
    Cooking oil

In skillet cook first 3 ingredients in margarine till tender; remove vegetables from skillet. Cook livers in same skillet 5 minutes; remove and chop. Combine livers, celery mixture, rice, tomatoes, ¾ teaspoon salt, sage, and ⅛ teaspoon pepper. Loosely stuff body and neck cavities of chickens; truss. Place birds, breast up, on rack in shallow roasting pan. Rub skin generously with oil. Roast, uncovered, at 375° for 1½ to 2 hours. Brush occasionally with pan drippings. Makes 8 servings.

FOIL-BAKED CHICKEN

  ⅓ cup each catsup and vinegar
  ¼ cup brown sugar
  ¼ cup margarine or butter, melted
  2 tablespoons Worcestershire sauce
  2 tablespoons lemon juice
  2 teaspoons each salt, paprika, chili
     powder, and dry mustard
  2 2½- to 3-pound ready-to-cook
     broiler-fryer chickens, cut up

Combine all ingredients *except* chickens. Add ½ cup water. Dip chickens in sauce. Divide chickens in 8 serving-sized portions, placing each portion on a separate piece of heavy foil. Pour 1 tablespoon sauce over each portion; seal foil securely. Bake at 400° for 45 minutes. Open packets; brush with remaining sauce. Bake 15 minutes more. Makes 8 servings.

LEMON-SAUCED FISH

2 pounds frozen or fresh fish fillets
2 tablespoons margarine, melted
2 tablespoons finely chopped onion
2 tablespoons margarine
2 tablespoons all-purpose flour
2 chicken bouillon cubes
2 tablespoons snipped parsley
1 teaspoon grated lemon peel
    (optional)
3 tablespoons lemon juice

Thaw fish, if frozen. Cut in 8 portions. Place in single layer on greased rack of broiler pan. Brush *half* the melted margarine over fish. Broil 4 inches from heat 8 to 10 minutes, brushing with remaining melted margarine once during cooking.

Meanwhile, in saucepan cook onion in 2 tablespoons margarine till tender. Blend in flour. Stir in 1 cup water and bouillon cubes. Cook and stir till thickened and bubbly. Add parsley, lemon peel, lemon juice, and dash pepper; heat through. Remove fish to serving platter. Pour sauce over fish. Makes 8 servings.

BARBECUED FISH FILLETS

1 pound frozen or fresh fish fillets
⅓ cup chopped onion
⅓ cup chopped celery
2 tablespoons margarine or butter
1 8-ounce can tomato sauce (1 cup)
2 tablespoons brown sugar
1 tablespoon all-purpose flour
1 tablespoon lemon juice
½ teaspoon paprika
½ teaspoon chili powder
¼ teaspoon salt

Thaw fish, if frozen. In saucepan cook onion and celery in margarine till tender but not brown. Stir in remaining ingredients *except* fish. Simmer, uncovered, for 10 minutes. Cut fish crosswise into 4 portions; arrange in shallow baking pan. Spoon sauce over the fish. Bake, uncovered, at 350° for 25 to 30 minutes. Makes 4 servings.

FISH FOR VARIETY

These pointers will cut food costs and give your menus a needed change of pace:
● Use fresh or frozen fish often in your diet. Fish frequently costs less per serving than the more commonly used red meats.
● Purchase different fish varieties during the seasons when they are in greatest abundance. Fish market managers can guide you concerning seasonal availability.

CURRIED FISH FILLETS

2 16-ounce packages frozen fish
    fillets, partially thawed
    Paprika
½ cup chopped celery
¼ cup chopped onion
2 tablespoons cooking oil
3 cups dry bread cubes
⅛ teaspoon ground ginger
1 8-ounce can tomatoes
3 tablespoons margarine or butter
3 tablespoons all-purpose flour
¾ to 1 teaspoon curry powder
1½ cups reconstituted nonfat dry milk

Slice each fish block in half horizontally. Cut each rectangle in half crosswise. Thaw completely. Place in greased 15½x10½x1-inch baking pan. Season with salt and paprika. Cook celery and onion in hot oil till crisp-tender. Combine with bread, ½ teaspoon salt, ginger, and dash pepper. Drain tomatoes, reserving ⅓ cup liquid; cut up tomatoes. Toss tomatoes and liquid into stuffing. Place ⅓ cup stuffing atop each fish portion. Bake, uncovered, at 350° for 15 to 20 minutes.

In saucepan melt margarine. Blend in flour, ½ teaspoon salt, and curry powder. Add milk. Cook and stir till thickened. Spoon sauce over fish. Garnish with parsley, if desired. Makes 8 servings.

SALMON PINWHEELS

Filling spirals around biscuit dough—

- ½ **cup chopped celery**
- ¼ **cup chopped onion**
- ¼ **cup chopped green pepper**
- 2 **tablespoons margarine or butter**
- 1 **16-ounce can pink salmon, drained, bones and skin removed, and flaked**

• • •

- 2 **cups sifted all-purpose flour**
- 3 **teaspoons baking powder**
- ½ **teaspoon salt**
- ¼ **cup shortening**
- ¾ **cup reconstituted nonfat dry milk or fluid milk**
- 1 **10½-ounce can condensed cream of chicken soup**
- 3 **tablespoons reconstituted nonfat dry milk or fluid milk**
- 2 **teaspoons lemon juice**

In saucepan cook celery, onion, and green pepper in margarine till tender but not brown. Remove from heat. Toss salmon lightly with the vegetable mixture.

In bowl sift together flour, baking powder, and salt; cut in shortening till like coarse crumbs. Make well in mixture; add ¾ cup milk all at once. Stir just till dough follows fork around bowl. Turn the dough onto a lightly floured surface; knead gently 10 to 12 strokes. Roll to 12x8-inch rectangle. Spoon salmon mixture over dough to within ½ inch of edges; starting at long side, roll up jelly-roll fashion. Moisten edges with water and seal. Cut the dough in 1-inch slices; place on greased baking sheet. Bake the pinwheels at 400° till lightly browned, about 20 minutes.

Meanwhile, in saucepan combine soup, 3 tablespoons milk, and lemon juice. Cook and stir till mixture is smooth and heated through. Pass sauce with the salmon pinwheels. Makes 6 servings.

Curried Fish Fillets provide elegant dining with simplicity. Top serving-sized portions of the fish with a delicately seasoned stuffing, bake, and then grace each fish portion with a smooth curry-flavored sauce.

CHEESY EGG BAKE

Mustard adds zip—

  1 10½-ounce can condensed cream of
    chicken soup
  ¼ cup reconstituted nonfat dry milk
  2 teaspoons grated onion
  ½ teaspoon prepared mustard
  4 ounces process Swiss cheese,
    shredded (1 cup)
  6 eggs
  6 ½-inch-thick slices French bread,
    buttered and halved
    Snipped parsley

In saucepan combine first 4 ingredients;
cook and stir till heated through. Remove
from heat; stir in cheese till melted. Pour 1
cup sauce into 10x6x1¾-inch baking dish.
Break eggs atop sauce. Spoon remaining
sauce around eggs. Stand bread around
baking dish edges, crust up. Bake at 350°
till eggs are set, about 20 minutes. Sprinkle
with parsley. Serves 6.

CHEESE-RICE SQUARES

A custardlike casserole—

  ⅓ cup finely chopped celery
  ¼ cup finely chopped onion
  2 tablespoons margarine or butter
  2¼ cups cooked or leftover rice
  6 ounces sharp process American
    cheese, shredded (¾ cup)
  3 beaten eggs
  1¼ cups reconstituted nonfat dry milk
  2 tablespoons snipped parsley
  ½ teaspoon salt
    Paprika

Cook celery and onion in margarine till
tender. Toss together celery mixture, rice,
and cheese. Combine eggs, milk, parsley,
and salt; stir into rice mixture. Turn into a
10x6x1¾-inch baking dish; sprinkle with
paprika. Set baking dish in pan of hot water.
Bake the casserole at 350° till a knife inserted off-center comes out clean, 55 to 60
minutes. Makes 6 servings.

*Cheesy Egg Bake provides one-step cooking at its finest. The Swiss cheese-
and chicken-sauced eggs bake as the ring of French bread slices toasts.
Parsley is sprinkled on top before serving this brunch treasure.*

COMPARE EGG PRICES

Eggs are sold in several sizes from small to extra large. To get the most for your money, compare the price of these different sizes. If the price difference between two sizes is less than 7¢, the larger sized eggs are a better buy than the smaller sized eggs.

Add ham, potatoes, and vegetables to scrambled eggs for delectable Farmers' Breakfast. Besides being a hearty day starter, as its name implies, this dish tastes equally good at the noon or evening meal.

DILLED CHEESE CASSEROLE

2 tablespoons margarine or butter
3 tablespoons all-purpose flour
2 teaspoons prepared mustard
½ teaspoon salt
2 cups reconstituted nonfat dry milk
**   or fluid milk**
4 ounces sharp process American
**   cheese, shredded (1 cup)**
2 beaten egg yolks
1 cup macaroni, cooked and drained
 • • •
1 cup cream-style cottage cheese
½ cup finely chopped dill pickle
1 cup soft bread crumbs
2 tablespoons margarine or butter,
**   melted**

In saucepan melt the first 2 tablespoons margarine or butter; blend in all-purpose flour, prepared mustard, and salt. Add reconstituted nonfat dry milk or fluid milk. Cook and stir till thickened and bubbly. Add cheese; cook and stir till melted. Stir small amount of hot mixture into egg yolks; return to saucepan. Cook and stir till bubbly; add cooked macaroni.

  Combine cream-style cottage cheese and chopped dill pickle. Spread *half* the macaroni mixture in a 10x6x1¾-inch baking dish; top with cottage cheese mixture and remaining macaroni mixture. Combine soft bread crumbs and melted margarine or butter; sprinkle atop casserole. Bake at 350° for 30 minutes. Makes 6 servings.

FARMERS' BREAKFAST

⅓ cup chopped onion
¼ cup chopped green pepper
¼ cup margarine or butter
½ 12-ounce can chopped ham,
**   cut in thin strips**
2 medium potatoes, cooked, peeled,
**   and cubed**
¾ teaspoon salt
6 beaten eggs

In skillet cook onion and green pepper in margarine till crisp-tender. Add ham, potatoes, and ¼ *teaspoon* salt; cook over medium heat for 10 minutes, stirring occasionally. Combine eggs, 2 tablespoons water, remaining salt, and dash pepper; pour over ham mixture. Cook over low heat, turning occasionally, till eggs are set. Trim with parsley, if desired. Serves 6.

SATISFYING BUDGET-STRETCHERS

MOCK LASAGNE CASSEROLE

As shown opposite section introduction—

> 1 pound bulk pork sausage
> 1 15-ounce can tomato sauce (2 cups)
> ½ teaspoon each garlic salt, pepper, and dried basil leaves, crushed
> 1 7-ounce package macaroni, cooked and drained
> 1½ cups cream-style cottage cheese
> 6 ounces process American cheese, shredded (1½ cups)

Brown the meat; drain off fat. Add tomato sauce, garlic salt, pepper, basil, and ½ cup water. Cover; simmer 15 minutes, stirring occasionally. In a 2-quart casserole layer *half each* macaroni, cottage cheese, shredded cheese, and meat sauce. Repeat. Bake at 375° for 30 minutes. Serves 6 to 8.

HAM-STUFFED POTATOES

Bake 6 large potatoes at 425° for 45 to 60 minutes; halve lengthwise. Scoop out insides; cube. Reserve potato shells. Cook ½ cup chopped onion and ½ cup chopped celery in 2 tablespoons margarine till tender. Add 2 cups diced, fully cooked ham, ¼ teaspoon garlic powder, and ¼ teaspoon salt. Cover; simmer 10 minutes.

Melt ¼ cup margarine. Blend in ¼ cup all-purpose flour. Stir in 2 cups reconstituted nonfat dry milk or fluid milk. Cook and stir till thickened and bubbly. Add ¼ cup chili sauce. Add ham mixture and cubed potatoes. Spoon into potato shells; arrange in a 13½x8¾x1¾-inch baking dish. Mix 3 tablespoons fine dry bread crumbs, ½ teaspoon paprika, and 1 tablespoon melted margarine; top shells. Bake, uncovered, at 350° for 30 minutes. Serves 6.

SAVORY CHICKEN PIES

Ideal for leftover chicken—

> ½ pound bulk pork sausage
> ¼ cup margarine or butter
> ⅓ cup all-purpose flour
> ¼ teaspoon salt
> ⅛ teaspoon pepper
> 1 13¾-ounce can chicken broth (1¾ cups)
> ⅔ cup reconstituted nonfat dry milk or fluid milk
> • • •
> 2 cups cubed, cooked or leftover chicken
> 1 10-ounce package frozen peas, thawed
> Savory Pastry

In saucepan brown sausage, breaking into pieces; drain on paper toweling. Pour off fat. In same saucepan melt margarine or butter. Blend in flour, salt, and pepper. Stir in chicken broth and milk. Cook and stir till thickened and bubbly; cook 1 minute more. Add browned sausage, cubed chicken, and thawed peas; heat through. Divide mixture among six 1-cup casseroles. Top with Savory Pastry. Place casseroles on baking sheet. Bake at 425° for 25 to 30 minutes. Makes 6 servings.

Savory Pastry: Combine 1 cup sifted all-purpose flour, 1 teaspoon celery seed, ½ teaspoon salt, and ½ teaspoon paprika; cut in ⅓ cup shortening. Sprinkle with 2 tablespoons water, a tablespoon at a time, mixing with fork till all flour is moistened and dough clings together. Gather dough together; press into ball. Roll ⅛ inch thick on lightly floured surface. Cut into 6 circles the size of the casseroles. Cut slits near center of each circle; place one pastry circle on top of each casserole.

Introduce a different look and flavor to a meat pie classic. For Savory Chicken Pies, fill individual casseroles with a mixture of sausage and the traditional chicken, peas, and gravy. Then, top with pastry wheels.

GOLD NUGGET MEAT PIE

1 16-ounce can tomatoes
1 beaten egg
2 cups soft bread crumbs (2 slices)
3 tablespoons catsup
2 tablespoons finely chopped onion
½ teaspoon Worcestershire sauce
1 pound ground beef
¼ cup chopped onion
2 tablespoons margarine or butter
1 12-ounce can whole kernel corn,
   drained
½ teaspoon dried basil leaves,
   crushed

Drain tomatoes, reserving ⅓ cup juice. Cut up tomatoes; set aside. Combine reserved tomato juice, next 5 ingredients, and ½ teaspoon salt. Add meat; mix well. Line bottom and sides of 9-inch pie plate with meat mixture, pressing lightly. Bake at 350° for 20 minutes.

Cook ¼ cup onion in margarine till tender. Add tomatoes, corn, and basil; mix. Remove meat from oven; drain off excess fat. Fill pie with corn mixture. Bake 15 to 20 minutes more. Serves 6.

CHEESE-TOMATO BAKE

4 medium tomatoes, peeled
1 teaspoon sugar
   Dash pepper
8 ounces sharp process American
   cheese, shredded (2 cups)
½ cup finely chopped celery
¼ cup finely chopped onion
1 cup soft bread crumbs
2 tablespoons margarine, melted

Slice tomatoes into fourths. Sprinkle with sugar and pepper. In bowl toss together cheese, celery, and onion. Place *half* of the tomato slices in 10x6x1¾-inch baking dish. Sprinkle *half* of the cheese mixture over tomato slices in baking dish. Repeat layers. Toss crumbs with margarine; sprinkle over casserole mixture. Bake at 350° for 25 to 30 minutes. Makes 6 servings.

FRANK AND KRAUT STEW

1 large onion, sliced
2 tablespoons margarine or butter
1 16-ounce can sauerkraut, undrained
   and snipped
1 16-ounce can tomatoes, cut up
3 medium potatoes, peeled and
   cubed (3 cups)
2 large carrots, diced (1½ cups)
1 cup water
2 tablespoons brown sugar
1 chicken bouillon cube
1 teaspoon salt
⅛ teaspoon pepper
1 pound frankfurters, quartered

In Dutch oven cook onion in margarine till tender. Add sauerkraut, tomatoes, potatoes, carrots, water, sugar, bouillon cube, salt, and pepper. Simmer, covered, till tender, about 45 minutes; stir occasionally. Add frankfurters; simmer, covered, about 5 minutes. Makes 9 or 10 servings.

FRIED GRITS WITH HAM

½ teaspoon salt
1 cup quick-cooking hominy grits
1½ cups finely diced, fully cooked ham
1 tablespoon margarine or butter
1 egg
¼ cup all-purpose flour
   Shortening
   Maple-flavored syrup

In saucepan combine 4 cups water and salt; bring to boiling. Slowly stir in grits. Cook, covered, over low heat for 2½ to 5 minutes, stirring occasionally; remove from heat. Stir in ham and margarine. Pour into a greased 8x8x2-inch pan. Cool; chill till firm, about 3 hours.

Cut in 2-inch squares. Beat egg with 2 tablespoons cold water; dip squares in egg mixture, then in flour. In skillet cook grit squares on both sides in small amount of hot shortening till golden brown, about 8 to 10 minutes. Serve with maple-flavored syrup. Makes 4 servings.

HAM AND MAC BAKE

 1 6-ounce package elbow macaroni
     (1⅔ cups)
 ¼ cup margarine or butter
 ¼ cup all-purpose flour
 2 tablespoons prepared mustard
 ¼ teaspoon salt
    Dash pepper
 2 cups reconstituted nonfat dry milk
 2 tablespoons brown sugar
 2 cups cubed, fully cooked ham
 2 medium apples, peeled and thinly
     sliced (2 cups)
 1 cup soft bread crumbs (1¼ slices)
 2 tablespoons margarine, melted

Cook macaroni in boiling, salted water till tender, 8 to 10 minutes; drain. In large saucepan melt ¼ cup margarine; blend in flour, mustard, salt, and pepper. Add milk all at once. Stir in sugar. Cook and stir till thickened and bubbly. Stir in macaroni, ham, and apple. Turn into 2-quart casserole. Combine crumbs and melted margarine; sprinkle over casserole. Bake at 350° for 30 to 35 minutes. Serves 8.

BEAN AND MEAT BAKE

 1 12-ounce can luncheon meat
 ¼ cup maple-flavored syrup
 1 21-ounce can pork and beans in
     tomato sauce
 ¼ cup chopped onion
 1 tablespoon all-purpose flour
 1 teaspoon prepared mustard
 1 ounce sharp process American
     cheese, shredded (¼ cup)

Cut luncheon meat into 8 slices; brush each slice with syrup, reserving remaining syrup. Arrange meat slices around edge of a 9-inch pie plate. In saucepan combine beans, remaining syrup, onion, flour, and mustard. Cook and stir till thickened and bubbly; pour boiling bean mixture into pie plate. Sprinkle with cheese. Bake at 350° till meat is lightly browned, about 20 minutes. Makes 4 servings.

 PASTA POINTERS

Fancy shapes of pasta may cost slightly more than the common elbow macaroni or plain spaghetti. However, using a fancy pasta is still one of the least expensive ways to make an ordinary dish seem special.

CHEESEBURGER BAKE

 4 ounces lasagne noodles (4 noodles)
 1 pound ground beef
 ½ teaspoon salt
 ½ teaspoon Worcestershire sauce
        • • •
 2 tablespoons margarine or butter
 ¼ cup chopped onion
 ¼ cup chopped green pepper
 2 tablespoons all-purpose flour
 ½ teaspoon salt
 1 cup reconstituted nonfat dry
     milk or fluid milk
 4 ounces sharp process American
     cheese (4 slices)

Cook lasagne noodles in boiling, salted water for 20 minutes; drain. Combine meat, ½ teaspoon salt, and Worcestershire sauce; mix well. Shape into 6 thin patties; brown in skillet. Remove patties; drain off fat.

 In skillet melt margarine or butter. Add onion and green pepper; cook till tender but not brown. Blend in flour and ½ teaspoon salt. Add milk all at once; cook and stir till thickened and bubbly.

 Cut 3 slices cheese into small pieces. In a 10x6x1¾-inch baking dish, layer 2 cooked noodles, *half* the white sauce, and *half* the cut-up cheese. Repeat with remaining noodles, sauce, and cut-up cheese. Top with browned meat patties. Bake at 350° for 20 minutes. Cut remaining cheese slice into 6 small triangles; place one triangle atop each meat patty. Bake 2 minutes more. Makes 6 servings.

MEATBALL-LIMA STEW

1 cup large dry lima beans
¼ cup all-purpose flour
1 8-ounce can tomatoes, cut up
1 cup sliced celery
1 cup sliced carrot
½ cup chopped onion
1 bay leaf
¼ cup fine dry bread crumbs
¼ cup reconstituted nonfat dry milk
¼ teaspoon Worcestershire sauce
1 pound ground beef

Rinse beans; place in Dutch oven. Add 4½ cups cold water. Bring to boiling; boil 2 minutes. Cover; let stand 1 hour. Do not drain. Combine flour and ½ cup cold water. Stir into beans; cook till thickened. Add vegetables, bay leaf, and 2 teaspoons salt. Bring to boiling. Cover; bake at 375° for 1½ hours, stirring occasionally.

Meanwhile, combine bread crumbs, milk, ½ teaspoon salt, and Worcestershire; mix into ground beef. Shape into small meatballs; add to stew. Cover; continue baking 45 minutes. Remove bay leaf. Serves 6.

TURKEY-VEGETABLE SOUP

1 meaty turkey frame
1 medium onion, chopped
1 teaspoon Worcestershire sauce
½ teaspoon dried sage leaves, crushed
1 bay leaf
1 17-ounce can whole kernel corn, drained
1 cup each sliced celery, sliced carrot, and diced turnip
2 tablespoons snipped parsley

Break frame to fit Dutch oven. Add 8 cups water, onion, 2 teaspoons salt, Worcestershire, sage, and bay leaf. Cover; simmer 1½ hours. Remove turkey frame; cut off meat and dice. Return meat to kettle; add vegetables and parsley. Cover; simmer 45 minutes, stirring occasionally. Remove bay leaf. Makes 8 to 10 servings.

PEA SOUP WITH DUMPLINGS

2¼ cups green split peas (1 pound)
1 meaty ham bone or 2 ham hocks (1½ pounds)
8 cups cold water
1 medium onion, sliced
1 cup diced celery
1 cup diced carrots
1 teaspoon salt
¼ teaspoon pepper
• • •
2 cups sifted all-purpose flour
3 teaspoons baking powder
1 teaspoon salt
3 tablespoons shortening
1 cup reconstituted nonfat dry milk or fluid milk
1 beaten egg

In Dutch oven combine green split peas, ham bone or ham hocks, cold water, sliced onion, diced celery, diced carrots, 1 teaspoon salt, and pepper. Bring to boiling; cover and simmer for 1½ hours, stirring occasionally. Remove ham bone or hocks; cut off meat and dice. Discard bone; add meat to soup in Dutch oven. Simmer, uncovered, 15 to 20 minutes more.

Meanwhile, sift together all-purpose flour, baking powder, and 1 teaspoon salt; cut in shortening. Combine reconstituted nonfat dry milk or fluid milk and beaten egg; add to dry mixture, stirring just till all ingredients are moistened. Drop batter from rounded tablespoon atop *bubbling* soup, making 16 to 18 dumplings. (Dip spoon into hot soup before spooning each dumpling to prevent sticking.) Cover tightly; let soup return to boiling. Reduce heat; simmer 15 to 18 minutes (do not lift cover). Makes 8 servings.

No-watch stew

Meatball-Lima Stew needs little of your attention →
as it cooks in the oven. When the bean and vege-
table base is two-thirds done, you simply add bite-
sized meatballs to make it a meal-in-one dish.

BEEF-BARLEY SOUP

 1 2-pound beef shank
 ¼ cup diced celery
 2 tablespoons snipped parsley
 1 tablespoon salt
 2 teaspoons Worcestershire sauce
 1 bay leaf
 ¼ teaspoon dried thyme leaves,
     crushed
 ½ cup pearl barley
 1 cup diced turnip
 1 cup sliced carrots
 ½ cup chopped onion
 ½ teaspoon Kitchen Bouquet (optional)

In Dutch oven combine first 7 ingredients and 8 cups water. Cover; bring to boiling. Reduce heat; simmer 2 hours. Remove bones; cut off meat and dice. Set meat aside. Strain broth; skim off excess fat. Return broth to pan with barley. Simmer, covered, for 30 minutes. Add meat, turnip, carrots, and onion; simmer, covered, till vegetables are tender, 30 minutes. Season to taste with salt and pepper. Stir in Kitchen Bouquet. Makes 6 to 8 servings.

PINTO BEAN SOUP

 1¼ cups dry pinto beans (8 ounces)
 1 1-pound beef shank
 1 ¾-pound ham hock
 1 small onion, thinly sliced
 ¼ teaspoon dried thyme leaves,
     crushed
 2 medium potatoes, peeled and diced
 2 medium carrots, sliced (1 cup)

Rinse beans; place in Dutch oven with 4 cups cold water. Bring to boiling; simmer for 2 minutes. Remove from heat; let stand 1 hour. Add beef shank, ham hock, onion, 1½ teaspoons salt, thyme, and dash pepper; return to heat and bring to boiling. Cover; simmer 1½ hours, stirring occasionally. Remove bones; cut off meat and dice. Add meat, potatoes, and carrots to soup. Cover; simmer 30 minutes. Season to taste with salt and pepper. Serves 6 to 8.

NICOISE SALAD

 ½ cup salad oil
 2 tablespoons vinegar
 2 tablespoons lemon juice
 2 teaspoons sugar
 1 teaspoon paprika
 1 teaspoon prepared mustard
 ½ teaspoon salt
 1 medium head lettuce, torn in bite-
     sized pieces
 1 16-ounce can whole or cut green
     beans, drained
 2 cups diced, peeled, cooked potatoes
 1 6½- or 7-ounce can tuna, drained
     and broken up
 2 medium tomatoes, peeled and sliced
 2 hard-cooked eggs, cut in wedges
     (optional)

In screw-top jar combine salad oil, vinegar, lemon juice, sugar, paprika, prepared mustard, and salt; cover and shake until thoroughly blended. Chill.

Just before serving, arrange lettuce in salad bowl. Shake dressing again and drizzle a few tablespoons over lettuce. Arrange beans, potatoes, tuna, and tomatoes atop lettuce. Garnish with egg wedges. Season with salt and pepper. Pour remaining dressing over salad. Serves 6.

BEEF SUPPER SALAD

 ½ cup salad dressing or mayonnaise
 2 tablespoons chopped dill pickle
 1 tablespoon catsup
 1 tablespoon prepared mustard
 ½ teaspoon salt
 2 cups cubed, cooked or leftover beef
 1 16-ounce can kidney beans, drained
 1 cup sliced celery
 ⅓ cup finely chopped onion
 2 hard-cooked eggs, chopped

Combine salad dressing, pickle, catsup, mustard, and salt. In bowl combine beef, kidney beans, celery, onion, and eggs. Pour salad dressing over bean mixture; toss lightly. Chill. Makes 5 servings.

Make Nicoise Salad a part of your menu repertoire during the summer when fresh tomatoes are in greatest abundance and lowest in price. For extra savings, replace the whole green beans with cut ones.

Flecks of carrot, celery, and onion add crunch to lightly dressed Rice and Tuna Salad. If you're looking for a good leftover idea, substitute cooked chicken or turkey pieces for the tuna.

RICE AND TUNA SALAD

2 cups cooked or leftover rice
1 6½- or 7-ounce can tuna, drained and broken up
1 cup shredded carrot
1 cup diced celery
2 tablespoons chopped onion
1 cup salad dressing or mayonnaise
1 teaspoon curry powder
2 teaspoons lemon juice
¼ teaspoon salt
  Carrot curls
  Parsley sprigs

Combine rice, tuna, carrot, celery, and onion; toss lightly. Chill. Combine salad dressing, curry powder, lemon juice, and salt; mix until well blended. Chill. To serve, toss mayonnaise mixture with tuna mixture. Garnish with carrot curls and parsley. Makes 4 servings.

CHEF'S RICE SALAD

1½ cups cooked or leftover rice
1 10-ounce package frozen peas, cooked and drained, or 1 17-ounce can peas, drained
¾ cup salad dressing or mayonnaise
¼ cup chopped dill pickle
1 tablespoon dill pickle juice
1 teaspoon grated onion
  Dash pepper
  • • •
  Lettuce
1 12-ounce can luncheon meat, cut in thin strips (2 cups)

Combine rice, peas, salad dressing, pickle, pickle juice, onion, and pepper; toss together lightly. Chill. To serve, line 4 individual salad plates with lettuce. Spoon the rice mixture onto lettuce; top with meat strips. Makes 4 servings.

HOT BEEF-POTATO SALAD

6 medium potatoes
1 3-ounce package sliced smoked beef, snipped
½ cup chopped onion
⅓ cup chopped green pepper
3 tablespoons margarine or butter
1 10½-ounce can condensed cream of celery soup
⅓ cup reconstituted nonfat dry milk or fluid milk
2 tablespoons vinegar
½ teaspoon salt
2 ounces process American cheese, shredded (½ cup)

Cook potatoes in boiling, salted water till tender; drain, peel, and dice (about 6 cups). Keep potatoes warm. In skillet cook beef, onion, and green pepper in margarine till vegetables are tender but not brown. Blend in soup, milk, vinegar, and salt. Gently stir in warm potatoes. Heat through. Sprinkle cheese atop potato mixture; cover and heat just till cheese begins to melt, about 3 or 4 minutes. Makes 6 servings.

TUNA AND SALMON BONUSES

Canned tuna and salmon are priced just right for families watching their food budgets. Use these tips to stretch your money without losing nutrition or appeal:

● Choose the tuna that best fits your needs. Tuna prices are determined by the type of tuna and the pack. "White" tuna is more costly than "light" tuna. The fancy- or solid-pack style of tuna commands the highest price, followed by chunk, flaked, and grated styles.

● Save on salmon by comparing salmon varieties. The redder the flesh, the higher the price. From reddest to pinkest are Sockeye, King, Silver, Pink, and Chum.

TANGY CHICKEN BOWL

    6 cups torn lettuce
    1 16-ounce can kidney beans, drained
 1½ cups cooked or leftover chicken,
        cut in strips
    2 ounces process American cheese,
        cut in strips (½ cup)
  ½ small cucumber, sliced
  ½ cup vinegar
  ⅓ cup sugar
    2 teaspoons grated onion
  ½ teaspoon salt
  ½ teaspoon celery seed
  ½ teaspoon dry mustard
  ¼ teaspoon paprika
    1 cup salad oil

In bowl arrange lettuce, beans, chicken, cheese, and cucumber; chill. In mixer bowl or blender container combine vinegar, sugar, onion, salt, celery seed, mustard, and paprika. Gradually add oil, beating or blending constantly. Chill. To serve, shake dressing well. Pour enough dressing over salad to moisten; toss lightly. Pass remaining dressing. Serves 10.

SALMON-MACARONI SALAD

Another time use tuna—

  ¾ cup elbow macaroni
    1 7¾-ounce can pink salmon,
        drained, bones and skin removed,
        and flaked
    1 cup finely shredded cabbage
    2 hard-cooked eggs, chopped
  ¾ cup salad dressing or mayonnaise
    2 tablespoons prepared mustard
    1 tablespoon lemon juice
  ¼ teaspoon salt

Cook macaroni according to package directions; drain. Combine macaroni, salmon, cabbage, and eggs. Blend salad dressing, mustard, lemon juice, and salt; toss lightly with salmon mixture. Chill. Serves 4.

HAM-VEGETABLE TOSS

    4 cups torn lettuce
    1 10-ounce package frozen corn,
        cooked and drained, or 1 17-
        ounce can whole kernel corn,
        drained
    1 10-ounce package frozen lima
        beans, cooked and drained, or 1
        16-ounce can green lima beans,
        drained
    1 12-ounce can chopped ham, cubed
    1 small onion, sliced and separated
        into rings
  ½ cup chopped celery
  ¼ cup chopped dill pickle
  ¼ cup salad oil
    2 tablespoons vinegar
    2 tablespoons catsup
    1 teaspoon prepared mustard
  ¾ teaspoon chili powder
  ½ teaspoon salt
  ¼ teaspoon sugar

In salad bowl combine first 7 ingredients; chill. In screw-top jar combine remaining ingredients; cover and shake well. Chill. Just before serving, shake dressing and toss with salad mixture. Makes 8 servings.

Try this easy version of a south-of-the-border favorite. For Mexi-Taco Sandwiches, heap a well-seasoned ground beef mixture onto hamburger bun halves, then pile on lettuce, tomato, and cheese.

MEXI-TACO SANDWICHES

 1 pound ground beef
½ cup chopped onion
 1 8-ounce can tomato sauce (1 cup)
 1 teaspoon Worcestershire sauce
¼ teaspoon salt
¼ teaspoon chili powder
⅛ teaspoon garlic powder
1½ cups corn chips, crushed
     (½ cup) (optional)
10 to 12 hamburger buns, split and
     toasted
½ medium head lettuce, shredded
     (3 cups)
 2 tomatoes, peeled and diced
 3 ounces sharp process American
     cheese, shredded (¾ cup)
Bottled hot pepper sauce (optional)

In skillet cook ground beef and onion till meat is browned and onion is tender. Add tomato sauce, Worcestershire sauce, salt, chili powder, and garlic powder; mix well and simmer 10 minutes.

Fold in crushed corn chips. Immediately spoon mixture onto bottom halves of buns. Top with lettuce, tomato, cheese, and tops of buns. Pass bottled hot pepper sauce, if desired. Makes 10 to 12 sandwiches.

QUICK BLINTZ SANDWICHES

1½ cups cream-style cottage cheese,
     drained
 1 egg
 2 tablespoons sugar
12 slices bread
 3 beaten eggs
⅓ cup reconstituted nonfat dry
     milk or fluid milk
Margarine or butter
Jelly or jam

Beat together cottage cheese, 1 egg, and sugar. Spread about ¼ cup filling on each of 6 bread slices. Top with remaining bread. Combine the 3 eggs and milk; dip sandwiches into egg mixture. Brown sandwiches on both sides in margarine or butter on griddle or in a skillet. Serve with jelly or jam. Makes 6 sandwiches.

BEEF-CABBAGE SANDWICHES

Try these in a lunch-box lunch—

 1 12-ounce can corned beef, flaked
1½ cups chopped cabbage
¼ cup chopped onion
¼ cup chopped dill pickle
¼ cup catsup
 2 tablespoons prepared mustard
18 slices bread
Margarine or butter

Combine corned beef, cabbage, onion, and pickle. Blend in catsup and mustard. Spread bread on 1 side with margarine Spread corned beef mixture on 9 slices bread. Top sandwiches with remaining bread, buttered side down. Serves 9.

CHEESE AND EGG PIZZA

1⅓ cups sifted all-purpose flour
2 teaspoons baking powder
3 tablespoons shortening
½ cup reconstituted nonfat dry milk
6 hard-cooked eggs, chopped
1 8-ounce can tomatoes, cut up
1 6-ounce can tomato paste
¼ cup chopped onion
¾ teaspoon dried oregano leaves, crushed
4 ounces sharp process American cheese, shredded (1 cup)
4 ounces process Swiss cheese, shredded (1 cup)

Sift together flour, baking powder, and ¼ teaspoon salt; cut in shortening till like coarse crumbs. Make a well in mixture; add milk. Stir just till dough follows fork around bowl. Turn onto lightly floured surface; knead 10 to 12 strokes. Roll dough to 12-inch circle; transfer to greased 12-inch pizza pan. Flute edges.

Sprinkle eggs over dough; season with salt and pepper. Combine tomatoes, tomato paste, onion, oregano, and ¼ teaspoon salt; spoon over eggs. Bake at 425° for 25 minutes. Toss cheeses together; sprinkle atop pizza. Bake till cheese melts, about 5 minutes. Makes one 12-inch pizza.

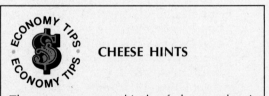

CHEESE HINTS

There are so many kinds of cheeses that it is difficult to know the one to buy. To get the most from what you spend, remember the following tips:
• Process cheese (blended fresh and aged) is less expensive than natural cheese.
• Process cheese has more cheese and less water than process cheese spread.
• It is more expensive to buy cheese already grated, shredded, or sliced.

CURRIED TURKEYWICHES

Chopped apple is mixed in—

1½ cups chopped, cooked or leftover turkey or chicken
½ cup chopped, peeled, tart apple
⅓ cup finely chopped celery
2 tablespoons finely chopped onion
2 tablespoons snipped parsley
½ cup salad dressing or mayonnaise
1 teaspoon curry powder
¼ teaspoon salt
Dash pepper
6 slices toast
Margarine or butter

Combine turkey, apple, celery, onion, and parsley. Blend together salad dressing or mayonnaise, curry powder, salt, and pepper. Add to turkey mixture; toss lightly.

Spread one side of toast slices with margarine. Arrange toast on baking sheet, margarine side up; divide and spoon turkey mixture over toast. Broil 4 to 6 inches from heat till heated through and lightly browned, about 4 to 5 minutes. Makes 6.

HASHBURGERS

1 16-ounce can corned beef hash
2 tablespoons finely chopped onion
2 tablespoons finely chopped dill pickle
2 teaspoons prepared mustard
¼ teaspoon Worcestershire sauce
6 slices sharp process American cheese
3 hamburger buns, split and toasted

Cut corned beef hash into six slices; place on ungreased baking sheet. Broil 4 to 5 inches from heat for 5 minutes. Meanwhile, combine onion, pickle, mustard, and Worcestershire sauce; spread mixture on hash slices. Cut cheese slices in half; stack two halves atop each hash slice. Return to broiler just till cheese begins to melt, about 1 minute. Serve open-face on toasted bun halves. Makes 6 sandwiches.

SKILLET HASH

In skillet heat 2 tablespoons margarine with 2 teaspoons prepared horseradish and 1 teaspoon Worcestershire sauce; add 1 large carrot, shredded, and ⅓ cup chopped onion. Cook till vegetables are tender. Add 2 cups chopped, cooked or leftover beef or pork; 2 cups chopped, peeled, cooked potatoes; ⅓ cup water; ½ teaspoon salt; and dash pepper. Cover and simmer till heated through, 15 minutes; stir occasionally. Stir in 1 cup canned or leftover gravy; heat through. Serves 6.

Mask the identity of leftover meat by preparing this Indian-inspired dish, Curried Ham in Popovers. Cooked chicken or turkey cubes can easily replace the ham in the curry sauce if you so desire.

CURRIED HAM IN POPOVERS

    2 tablespoons chopped green pepper
    1 tablespoon chopped onion
    1 tablespoon margarine or butter
    1 10½-ounce can condensed cream of
        celery soup
    ⅓ cup salad dressing or mayonnaise
    ⅓ cup reconstituted nonfat dry milk
    ¼ to ½ teaspoon curry powder
    2 cups cubed, fully cooked
        or leftover ham
    Popovers

Cook vegetables in margarine till tender. Stir in next 5 ingredients; cook and stir till heated through. Serve in hot Popovers, split lengthwise. Serves 6.

Popovers: Place 2 eggs in mixer bowl; add 1 cup reconstituted nonfat dry milk, 1 cup sifted all-purpose flour, and ½ teaspoon salt. Beat 1½ minutes with rotary beater or electric mixer. Add 1 tablespoon cooking oil; beat 30 seconds more. Fill 6 well-greased 5-ounce custard cups half full. Bake at 475° for 15 minutes. Reduce heat to 350°; bake till browned and firm, 25 to 30 minutes. A few minutes before removing from oven, prick with fork.

CHICKEN SPOON BREAD

    ½ cup yellow or white cornmeal
    1 tablespoon all-purpose flour
    1 cup chicken broth
    1 cup reconstituted nonfat dry milk
    2 tablespoons margarine or butter
    2 beaten egg yolks
    1½ cups chopped, cooked or leftover
        chicken
    2 stiffly beaten egg whites

In saucepan mix cornmeal, flour, and ¼ teaspoon salt; stir in broth and milk. Cook and stir till thickened and bubbly; cook and stir 2 minutes more. Remove from heat; stir in margarine. Cool slightly. Stir in yolks and chicken; fold in whites. Pour into greased 1-quart casserole. Bake, uncovered, at 325° for 1 hour. Serves 6.

BEEF PANCAKE ROLL-UPS

1 cup sifted all-purpose flour
½ teaspoon salt
1 cup reconstituted nonfat dry milk
2 beaten eggs
  Shortening
1 cup finely chopped celery
2 tablespoons margarine or butter
2 cups chopped, cooked or leftover
  beef
1 10½-ounce can condensed cream of
  mushroom soup
2 tablespoons margarine or butter
2 tablespoons all-purpose flour
1 cup reconstituted nonfat dry milk
2 ounces sharp process American
  cheese, shredded (½ cup)
1 teaspoon prepared mustard
  Paprika

Sift together 1 cup flour and salt; add 1 cup milk and eggs. Beat smooth. Lightly grease a 6-inch skillet with shortening; heat. Remove from heat; add 3 tablespoons batter. Rotate pan to spread batter. Return to heat; brown on one side only. Invert onto paper toweling. Repeat, making 8 pancakes; grease pan occasionally.

Cook celery in 2 tablespoons margarine till tender; remove from heat. Stir in meat and *half* of the soup. Spoon about ¼ cup meat mixture in center of *each* pancake, unbrowned side up. Roll up; place in one layer in 11¾x7½x1¾-inch baking dish.

Melt 2 tablespoons margarine; blend in 2 tablespoons flour. Add 1 cup milk; cook and stir till thickened. Stir in cheese, mustard, and remaining soup till smooth; spoon over roll-ups. Sprinkle with paprika. Bake at 325° for 20 minutes. Serves 4.

USES FOR LEFTOVERS

Probably the most sensible and yet oft forgotten way to economize is to make sure that you never throw away good food. In other words, save both large and small amounts of leftovers and make wise use of them. Often, this means that you have to employ creativity to think up a use for the leftovers, especially when there's only a small amount. To help you out, here are some ways to put small amounts of various foods to good use.

Egg yolks (2 yolks = 1 whole egg)	Cream puddings and fillings, custards, sauces, eggnog, noodles, salad dressings, and scrambled eggs
Egg whites	Angel food cakes, fluffy frostings, fruit whips, meringues, candies, glazes, and foamy sauces
Hard-cooked eggs	Casseroles, salads, sandwiches, garnishes, and deviled eggs
Cooked meat, fish, and poultry	Casseroles, skillet dishes, creamed dishes, patties, meat pies, salads, sandwiches, pizzas, stuffed vegetables, and pancakes
Meat drippings	Gravies, casseroles, soups, stews, and sauces
Cooked potatoes	Fry, cream, use in croquettes, meat pie toppings, stews, soups
Fruits	Salads, fruit cups, sauces, quick or yeast breads, shortcakes, upside-down cakes, cobblers, and parfaits
Cooked cereals	Fry, use in meat loaves or patties, and use in sweet puddings
Cooked pastas	Casseroles, meat or cheese loaves, and salads
Dry bread	French toast, croutons, stuffings, crumb toppings and coatings
Soft bread	Bread puddings, meat loaves, and stuffings
Cakes or cookies	Brown betty, cottage pudding, crumb crusts, crumb toppings
Evaporated milk	(Dilute with equal parts of water to make whole milk) Puddings, cakes, cookies, casseroles, breads, candies, frozen desserts, gelatin salads, cream soups, cream fillings, and sauces
Vegetables	Salads, relishes, casseroles, soups, and stews

ECONOMICAL SIDE DISHES

Are you short on ideas for what to serve with the main dish? Then you'll especially welcome this myriad of meal-maker recipes that will revitalize your menus and your food allowance.

Select from the tempting salads, vegetables, and breads for new accompaniment ideas. Try a fruit, vegetable, or gelatin salad combination, or shake together a salad dressing for your favorite tossed salad. Another time, prepare one of the vegetable fix-ups. Don't forget that yeast and quick breads take on matchless eye- and flavor-appeal when you make them yourself.

For rousing meal finales or between-meal snacks, you'll also find luscious desserts that won't bruise your budget. Satisfy the family's sweet tooth with the old- and new-fashioned cakes, cookies, and fruit desserts.

Saucy Vegetables, Crusty Water Rolls, Pear-Banana-Lime Mold, and Choco-Cherry Cake Roll —choose one or more recipes to suit your menu.

LOW-COST SALADS

PEAR-BANANA-LIME MOLD

As shown opposite section introduction—

      ⅔ cup evaporated milk
      1 16-ounce can pear slices or halves
      1 3-ounce package lime-flavored
         gelatin
      2 ripe, medium bananas
      1 tablespoon lemon juice
      Lettuce

Pour milk into freezer tray. Freeze till edges are icy. Drain pears, reserving syrup. Add water to make 1 cup; bring to boil. Dissolve gelatin in boiling liquid. Chill till partially set. Gradually add milk to gelatin, whipping till double. Dice pears. Slice bananas; sprinkle with lemon juice. Fold fruits into gelatin. Pour the mixture into a 6½-cup ring mold. Chill mixture till firm. Unmold on lettuce. Serves 8.

SPICY PEACH MOLD

      1 16-ounce can peach slices
      ½ cup sugar
      2 tablespoons vinegar
      8 whole cloves
      ¼ teaspoon ground cinnamon
      1 8¾-ounce can crushed pineapple
      1 3-ounce package orange-flavored
         gelatin

Drain peaches, reserving syrup. Add water to syrup to make ¾ cup. In saucepan combine reserved syrup, sugar, vinegar, and spices; bring to boil. Add peaches; simmer, covered, 10 minutes. Drain pineapple, reserving syrup. Add water to syrup to make ¾ cup. Strain peaches, reserving hot syrup. Dissolve gelatin in hot peach syrup; add reserved pineapple syrup. Chill till partially set. Fold in fruit. Pour into 4½-cup mold. Chill till firm. Serves 6.

PEAS AND LETTUCE BOWL

Combine ⅓ cup sugar; ¼ cup vinegar; 2 tablespoons salad oil; 1 teaspoon salt; ½ teaspoon dry mustard; ½ teaspoon celery seed; ¼ teaspoon dried thyme leaves, crushed; and dash pepper. Mix thoroughly. Stir in two 10-ounce packages frozen peas, cooked and drained. Cover; chill.

In skillet melt 2 tablespoons margarine. Add 2 slices bread, cut in cubes; toast till crisp, turning occasionally. At serving time, divide 4 cups torn lettuce between 8 individual serving bowls. Separate 2 onion slices into rings. Top lettuce with peas, onion, and bread. Serves 8.

BLENDER MAYONNAISE

      1 large egg
      1 tablespoon vinegar
      ¼ teaspoon dry mustard
      ⅛ teaspoon paprika
      Dash cayenne
      1 cup salad oil
      1 tablespoon lemon juice

Put first 5 ingredients and ½ teaspoon salt in blender container; blend well. With blender running slowly, gradually add *half* the oil. (When necessary, stop blender and scrape down sides.) Add lemon juice. Slowly pour remaining oil into container running blender slowly. Makes 1¼ cups.

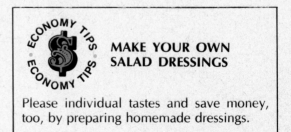

ECONOMY TIPS · ECONOMY TIPS ·

MAKE YOUR OWN SALAD DRESSINGS

Please individual tastes and save money, too, by preparing homemade dressings.

KIDNEY BEAN BOWL

Celery and apple add crunch—

  1 15-ounce can kidney beans, drained
  ½ cup sliced celery
  2 tablespoons chopped onion
  ¼ cup salad dressing or mayonnaise
  1 cup diced, unpeeled apple
  ⅓ cup diced process American cheese
    Lettuce

Combine beans, celery, onion, ¼ teaspoon salt, and dash pepper. Add salad dressing. Cover; chill. Stir in apple and cheese. Serve in lettuce-lined bowl. Serves 8.

POPPY SEED DRESSING

  ½ cup sugar
  2 teaspoons all-purpose flour
  2 teaspoons paprika
  ⅓ cup vinegar
  1 tablespoon lemon juice
  1 cup salad oil
  1½ teaspoons poppy seed

In saucepan combine sugar, flour, and paprika; add vinegar. Cook and stir till thickened and bubbly. Cook 1 minute. Add juice; cool. Slowly add oil, beating constantly with electric mixer. Stir in seed. Chill. Serve with fruit. Makes 1½ cups.

Combine diced apple, diced cheese, kidney beans, celery, onion, and salad dressing to create this intriguing salad, Kidney Bean Bowl. Line the salad bowl with lettuce before spooning in the salad mixture.

BARGAIN-PRICED VEGETABLES

SAUCY VEGETABLES

As pictured opposite section introduction—

    3 cups sliced, peeled potatoes
    1 10-ounce package frozen peas and
        carrots
    1 10½-ounce can condensed cream of
        mushroom soup
    3 ounces sharp process American
        cheese, shredded (¾ cup)
    ¼ cup reconstituted nonfat dry milk
    1 teaspoon prepared mustard

Cook potatoes and peas and carrots in small amount of boiling, salted water just till tender, 8 to 10 minutes. Drain. In saucepan combine remaining ingredients; heat and stir till cheese melts. Stir in vegetables; heat through. Serves 4 to 6.

MUSTARD-SAUCED CABBAGE

Horseradish and mustard add zip—

    1 small head cabbage, cut in 4
        wedges
    2 tablespoons finely chopped onion
    2 tablespoons margarine or butter
    1 tablespoon all-purpose flour
    ⅔ cup evaporated milk
    1 tablespoon prepared mustard
    2 teaspoons prepared horseradish

Cook cabbage wedges in small amount of boiling, salted water for 10 to 12 minutes; drain well. Meanwhile, in small saucepan cook onion in margarine till tender. Blend in flour, ¼ teaspoon salt, and dash pepper. Add milk and ½ cup water. Cook and stir till thickened and bubbly. Stir in mustard and horseradish. Spoon over cabbage. Top with snipped parsley, if desired. Serves 4.

VEGETABLE VALUES

Save on vegetables with these hints:
● Compare the price of all-purpose and baking potatoes before you buy. Usually, all-purpose potatoes are lower priced and can be used in all types of dishes.
● Check the price of large- versus small-sized packages. Large bags of frozen vegetables usually cost less per ounce. You can pour out just the amount you need and return the rest to the freezer.

MAPLE-GLAZED SQUASH

    2 acorn squash
    ⅔ cup maple-flavored syrup
    ½ cup soft bread crumbs
    ¼ cup margarine, softened

Trim ends of acorn squash, then cut crosswise into 1-inch slices; discard seeds. Season with salt and pepper. Arrange a single layer of squash in large shallow baking pan; cover and bake at 350° for 30 to 35 minutes. Combine syrup, crumbs, and margarine; spread over squash. Bake uncovered, for 15 to 20 minutes, basting occasionally. Makes 6 to 8 servings.

Tempting and tasty

Both piping-hot vegetables are cloaked with flavor- →
ful coatings. A piquant sauce is draped liberally over Mustard-Sauced Cabbage, while Maple-Glazed Squash is baked with maple-flavored syrup.

PENNY-WISE BREADS

CRUSTY WATER ROLLS

As shown opposite section introduction—

In large mixer bowl combine 1 package active dry yeast and 1¼ cups sifted all-purpose flour. Heat 1 cup water, 1 tablespoon sugar, 2 tablespoons shortening, and 1½ teaspoons salt just till warm. Add to dry mixture; add 2 egg whites. Beat at low speed with electric mixer for ½ minute, scraping constantly. Beat 3 minutes at high speed. By hand, stir in enough of 1¾ to 2 cups sifted all purpose flour to make a moderately soft dough.

Turn out onto floured surface; knead 8 to 10 minutes. Place in lightly greased bowl, turning once. Cover; let rise in warm place 50 to 60 minutes. Punch down; cover and let rest 10 minutes. Divide dough into 20 to 24 balls; shape into ovals. Place on greased baking sheet; with sharp knife, make a ⅛-inch-deep lengthwise slit across each top. Cover; let rise 30 to 40 minutes. Place large shallow pan on bottom oven rack; fill with boiling water. Bake rolls on rack above water at 450° for 10 to 12 minutes. Makes 20 to 24 rolls.

APPLESAUCE PUFFS

Sure to be a favorite—

Combine 2 cups packaged biscuit mix, ¼ cup sugar, and 1 teaspoon ground cinnamon. Combine 1 slightly beaten egg, ½ cup applesauce, and ¼ cup reconstituted nonfat dry milk; add to dry mixture and beat vigorously for 30 seconds. Fill greased muffin pans ⅔ full. Bake at 400° for 15 to 20 minutes. Cool slightly; remove from pans. Combine ¼ cup sugar and ¼ teaspoon ground cinnamon. Dip muffin tops in 2 tablespoons melted margarine or butter, then in sugar mixture. Makes 10 to 12.

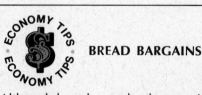

BREAD BARGAINS

Although breads may be the most inexpensive part of your diet, there are still some worthwhile ways to reduce their cost:
● Bake specialty breads at home. Ready-baked items from the store cost considerably more and may be less nutritious.
● Watch for mark-downs on day-old bread. You can buy now and freeze for later.
● Slowly oven-dry stale bread slices, whole or cubed. Crush slices for bread crumbs. The bread cubes, now croutons, are delicious in tossed salads.

THREE-FLOUR BREAD

    3¼ to 3½ cups sifted all-purpose flour
    2 packages active dry yeast
    1½ cups whole wheat flour
    ½ cup rye flour
    2 cups reconstituted nonfat dry milk
    ½ cup brown sugar
    2 tablespoons granulated sugar
    3 tablespoons shortening

Combine 1 cup all-purpose flour and next 3 ingredients. Heat milk, sugars, 1 tablespoon salt, and shortening. Add to flours. Beat at low speed of electric mixer for ½ minute, scraping constantly. Beat 3 minutes at high. Stir in enough of remaining all-purpose flour for a moderately stiff dough. Turn onto floured surface; knead 8 to 10 minutes. Place in greased bowl, turning once. Cover; let rise 1½ hours. Punch down; let rest 10 minutes. Shape into 2 loaves; place in 2 greased 8½x4½x2½-inch loaf dishes. Let rise 45 to 60 minutes. Bake at 375° for 40 minutes.

One bite from a slice of wholesome Three-Flour Bread will convince you that home-baked breads are well worth the extra effort. What's lost in time is gained in flavor, nutrition, and financial savings.

THRIFTY DESSERTS

CHOCO-CHERRY CAKE ROLL

As shown opposite section introduction —

4 egg yolks
¼ cup sugar
½ teaspoon red food coloring
• • •
4 egg whites
½ cup sugar
¾ cup sifted all-purpose flour
¼ cup unsweetened cocoa powder
1 teaspoon baking powder
¼ teaspoon salt
• • •
Sifted confectioners' sugar
Cherry Filling

Beat egg yolks till thick and lemon-colored; gradually beat in ¼ cup sugar. Add food coloring. Beat egg whites till soft peaks form; gradually add ½ cup sugar, beating till stiff peaks form. Fold yolks into whites. Sift together flour, cocoa, baking powder, and salt; fold into egg mixture. Spread batter evenly in greased and lightly floured 15½x10½x1-inch jelly roll pan. Bake at 375° till the cake is done, 10 to 12 minutes.

Immediately loosen sides and turn out on towel sprinkled with sifted confectioners' sugar. Starting at narrow end, roll cake and towel together; cool on rack. Unroll cake; spread with Cherry Filling. Roll up. Dust with additional confectioners' sugar, if desired. Makes ten 1-inch slices.

Cherry Filling: Drain one 16-ounce can pitted tart red cherries (water pack), reserving ¾ cup juice (if necessary, add water to make ¾ cup). In small saucepan combine ¾ cup sugar, 3 tablespoons cornstarch, and ¼ teaspoon salt; stir in reserved juice and ¼ teaspoon red food coloring. Cook over high heat, stirring constantly, till thickened and bubbly. Stir in drained cherries, 1 tablespoon margarine or butter, and 6 to 8 drops almond extract. Cool thoroughly.

PINEAPPLE-CUSTARD MOLD

An elegant dessert —

½ cup sugar
1 envelope unflavored gelatin
¼ teaspoon salt
¾ cup reconstituted nonfat dry milk
2 beaten egg yolks
½ teaspoon vanilla
½ cup evaporated milk
2 stiffly beaten egg whites
1 8¾-ounce can pineapple tidbits
⅓ cup sugar
4 teaspoons cornstarch
Dash salt
¾ cup orange juice

In small saucepan combine ½ cup sugar, gelatin, and ¼ teaspoon salt. Combine milk and egg yolks; add to gelatin mixture. Cook and stir over low heat till mixture thickens slightly and coats a metal spoon. Add vanilla. Chill till partially set.

Meanwhile, pour evaporated milk into freezer tray. Freeze till edges are icy; whip to stiff peaks. Fold whipped milk and whites into gelatin mixture. Turn into 4½-cup mold; chill till firm.

To prepare sauce, drain pineapple, reserving syrup. In saucepan combine ⅓ cup sugar, cornstarch, and dash salt. Stir in reserved syrup and orange juice. Cook and stir till thickened and bubbly. Reduce heat; cook 1 minute. Cool slightly; stir in pineapple. Chill. Unmold gelatin. Serve with sauce. Makes 8 servings.

Delicate and delicious

End the meal on a splendid note by presenting Pineapple-Custard Mold on a pedestal plate. Spoon some of the sunny pineapple sauce over the smooth, creamy custard. Then, pass the remaining sauce.

When it's snack time at your house, bring out the pitcher of ice-cold milk and the cookie jar filled with chewy, raisin-studded Applesauce-Oat Cookies. They are a favorite treat for young and old alike.

APPLESAUCE-OAT COOKIES

Especially good served warm—

In mixing bowl cream together 1 cup shortening, 1 cup brown sugar, and ½ cup granulated sugar till light and fluffy; beat in 2 eggs and 1 teaspoon vanilla. Add ¾ cup applesauce; mix well.

Sift together 1 cup sifted all-purpose flour, 1 teaspoon salt, 1 teaspoon ground cinnamon, ½ teaspoon baking powder, and ½ teaspoon baking soda. Add dry ingredients to applesauce mixture, mixing well. Stir in 4 cups quick-cooking rolled oats and 1½ cups raisins. Drop dough from teaspoon onto greased cookie sheet. Bake at 400° till the cookies are golden brown, 12 to 15 minutes. Makes about 7 dozen cookies.

SURPRISE PIE

The filling is oatmeal and coconut—

- ½ cup sugar
- ¼ cup margarine or butter, softened
- 1 cup dark or light corn syrup
- ¼ teaspoon salt
- 3 well-beaten eggs
- ½ cup shredded coconut
- ½ cup quick-cooking rolled oats
- 1 9-inch unbaked pastry shell

Add sugar gradually to margarine; cream till fluffy. Add syrup and salt; beat well. Beat in eggs, one at a time. Stir in coconut and oats. Pour into pastry shell. Bake at 350° till knife inserted off-center comes out clean, 50 minutes. Cool

PINEAPPLE CRUNCH CAKE

1 20-ounce can crushed pineapple
1 package 2-layer-size yellow cake mix
2 eggs
1 cup shredded coconut
⅔ cup brown sugar
6 tablespoons margarine, melted
2 teaspoons lemon juice

Drain pineapple, reserving syrup. Using the syrup as part of the liquid and the 2 eggs, prepare cake according to package directions. Pour into greased and floured 13x9x2-inch baking pan. Bake as directed. Combine pineapple and remaining ingredients; spread atop cake. Broil 4 to 5 inches from heat for 5 to 7 minutes.

LEMON-SPICE DIAMONDS

Cream ¾ cup shortening, 1⅓ cups brown sugar, and ½ teaspoon vanilla till fluffy. Add 2 eggs and 2 tablespoons lemon juice; beat well. Sift together 1 cup sifted all-purpose flour, 1 teaspoon baking powder, and ¼ teaspoon each ground cinnamon and ground nutmeg; add to sugar mixture. Add 1 cup quick-cooking rolled oats. Spread in greased 13x9x2-inch baking pan. Bake at 350° for 20 to 25 minutes. While warm, top with Glaze. Cool. Cut in diamonds.

Glaze: Combine 1½ cups sifted confectioners' sugar, 1 tablespoon lemon juice, and enough reconstituted nonfat dry milk to make of glaze consistency.

LEMONY CREAM PUFFS

½ cup margarine or butter
1 cup boiling water
1 cup sifted all-purpose flour
¼ teaspoon salt
4 eggs
½ cup shredded coconut
Lemon Filling

Melt margarine in boiling water. Add flour and salt; stir vigorously. Cook and stir till mixture forms ball that doesn't separate. Cool slightly. Add eggs, one at a time, beating after each till smooth. Stir in coconut. Drop by heaping tablespoons 3 inches apart on greased baking sheet. Bake at 450° for 15 minutes, then at 325° for 25 minutes. Remove from oven; split. Turn oven off; put puffs back in oven to dry, about 20 minutes. Cool. Fill with Lemon Filling. Makes 10.

Lemon Filling: In saucepan combine 1 cup sugar, ¼ cup cornstarch, and ⅛ teaspoon salt. Slowly stir in 1½ cups water. Cook and stir till thickened and bubbly. Stir a little hot mixture into 3 beaten egg yolks; return to hot mixture. Heat till bubbly; cook and stir 2 minutes. Remove from heat; stir in ⅓ cup lemon juice and ¼ cup margarine. Chill.

PASTRY SHELL

1½ cups sifted all-purpose flour
½ teaspoon salt
½ cup shortening
4 to 5 tablespoons cold water

Sift together flour and salt; cut in shortening till the size of small peas. Sprinkle 1 tablespoon water over part of the mixture. Gently toss with fork; push to side of bowl. Repeat till all is moistened. Form dough into ball; flatten on floured surface. Roll dough ⅛ inch thick. Fit pastry into pie plate; trim ½ to 1 inch beyond edge. Fold under and flute edges as desired.

To bake, prick bottom and sides with fork. Bake at 450° for 10 to 12 minutes.

MORE FOR YOUR MONEY

Need help in making the food budget work? If so (and who doesn't), this section will be extremely helpful with its medley of planning, spending, and preparation strategies.

To begin, use the information in Plan Before You Spend to learn where and how to improve your food plans. Take into account family food preferences, good food buys, nutritional needs, and storage facilities. Then, before you shop, examine the Shopper's Checklist of cost-cutting tips for ways to eliminate unnecessary expenses.

Likewise, refer frequently to Make the Most of Meals. Become familiar with economical meat cuts, using the identification sketches plus the buying and preparation information. Learn how to divide large roasts for several meals as well as how to cut poultry into serving pieces.

Speed up your planning sessions by organizing a special center in your kitchen where you can keep cook books, cost records, and other references.

PLAN BEFORE YOU SPEND

If the word "budget" conjures up thoughts of penny-pinching and dull routine, revise your thinking. A budget is simply planned spending. This means mental and written planning to use your food money for economical, yet pleasing and varied meals.

Although this may not sound hard, getting started on the new approach may be difficult. You'll probably find yourself asking "How do I plan?" Simple. Start with a realistic budget. Then, plan your menus and shopping around that budget.

Only you can decide when the budget is realistic. For example, family size influences the budget—more people mean more food. And if foods for special or restricted diets such as for the diabetic are required, food may cost you more.

MENU PLANNING

The best way to approach menu planning is to plan menus for at least several days at a time. Gather together newspaper food ads, cook books and recipes, and the Basic Four Food Guide. Then, consider nutrition, family preferences, current good food buys, preparation time, food on hand, and available storage space.

As a rule, you'll fulfill nutritional needs if you serve one food from each Basic Four food group at every meal. To cut costs and maintain nutrition, use these tips:

1. Consult the Basic Four sketches for economical foods that fall in each group.

2. Serve only average portions of meat. Many families eat meat that totals more than the 4 to 6 ounces needed daily.

3. Use meat-stretching dishes, such as casseroles and lower-cost meat substitutes such as dry beans, frequently.

4. To divert the family's attention from smaller meat servings, concentrate on making the rest of the meal enticing. For instance, serve a variety of fruits and vegetables, and try new homemade breads.

5. Make the dessert a nutritious part of the meal. A custard or cream pudding provides part of the day's milk requirement. Likewise, a peanut butter dessert adds protein to the meal.

Whenever you plan menus, consider the foods your family prefers. Luckily, most families have more likes than dislikes.

Some foods, such as ground beef, always tend to be economical. Others are seasonal or sale items only. To learn what foods are currently low-priced, consult the food ads and use the featured foods.

Often, savings must be equated in terms of time as well as money. Because most convenience foods are not budget foods, the less preparation time you have available, the more money you will usually need for timesaving foods.

The food you have on hand and the storage space available also affect your plans. If you have freezer space, purchase specials in larger quantities, but turn over the freezer supply at least once a year.

PLANNING FOR SHOPPING

A well-organized shopping list is important when trying to maintain a budget. Use these suggestions for your list:

1. Make out your shopping list from the menus and recipes you plan to use.

2. Put the advertised price and brand of sale items on your list.

3. Record the amount of food you need to buy by consulting recipes and the How Much To Buy chart inside the front cover.

4. Check the Unit Price Chart inside the back cover to compare the cost per pint or pound of different brands or sizes.

5. Plan to shop when you aren't hungry, when the shelves are well-stocked, and when the most specials are offered.

As a final check before you leave for the store, look over the Shopper's Checklist on page 88. Then, happy budgeting!

BASIC FOUR FOOD GUIDE

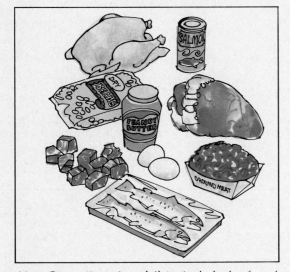

Meat Group (2 servings daily) — *Includes beef, veal, pork, lamb, poultry, fish, and eggs. Alternate sources include dry beans and peas, nuts, and peanut butter. Consider as 1 serving: 2 to 3 ounces cooked, lean meat, fish, or poultry; 2 eggs; 1 cup cooked dry beans or peas; or ¼ cup peanut butter.*

Milk Group (2 to 3 cups for children, 4 or more cups for teen-agers, 2 or more cups for adults) — *Includes milk, buttermilk, yogurt, ice cream, and cheese. Consider as calcium equivalents for 1 cup milk: 1 cup yogurt; 1⅓ ounces Cheddar-type cheese; 1½ cups cottage cheese; or 1 pint (2 cups) ice cream.*

Vegetable-Fruit Group (4 servings daily) — *Include 1 serving of citrus fruit or 2 servings of tomato daily and 1 serving of a dark green vegetable or deep yellow vegetable or fruit 3 to 4 times a week. Consider as 1 serving: ½ cup fruit or vegetable; 1 medium apple; or ½ grapefruit or cantaloupe.*

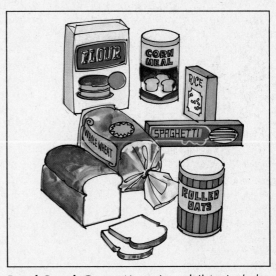

Bread-Cereal Group (4 servings daily) — *Includes breads, cereals, cornmeal, grits, crackers, pastas, and rice that are whole grain, enriched, or restored. Consider as 1 serving: 1 slice bread; ½ to ¾ cup cooked cereal, rice, macaroni, noodles, or spaghetti; or ¾ to 1 cup ready-to-eat cereal.*

SHOPPER'S CHECKLIST

1. Keep a week-to-week price list until you become familiar with regular food prices. Then you will be able to decide which "specials" are good buys.

2. Keep abreast of the monthly "plentiful foods" list supplied by the United States Department of Agriculture. Communications media such as newspapers, magazines, and radio and television stations usually publicize these lists.

3. Familiarize yourself with the more common can sizes. Some cans look similar in size, yet hold different amounts (see the Common Can Sizes chart).

4. Compare the cost of various forms of food—fresh, frozen, canned, and dried—using cost per serving. This is the most accurate comparison method because it takes inedible losses into account.

5. Read labels carefully, picking out the form, amount, grade, and ingredient listing as well as the price and net weight. Remember that ingredients are listed in descending order by weight, so you can afford to pay a little more for chicken with rice than for rice with chicken.

6. Try goods packaged under a private brand label. If they meet your quality needs, you can save money by using them.

7. Choose the grade and quality that fits your use. For example, when shape, uniformity of size, and color are not important, use the thriftiest form. You get equally good flavor and nutritive value.

8. Buy fresh fruits and vegetables during the season when the abundance is greatest and the price is the lowest.

9. Select foods that are traditionally or simply packaged. Fancy or extra packaging is generally more costly.

10. Select large in preference to small packages of staple foods if you use them often or in large quantities. You usually pay less per ounce, pound, or pint for the food in the large containers.

11. Take advantage of special sales by buying extras if you have the storage space (for meats, see page 92). If the special is a multiple price (5/$1.00), you don't have to buy all the packages.

12. Make use of "cents off" coupons for items that you normally buy. However, buying an item you don't need just because you have a coupon is no bargain.

13. For storing foods, choose the best, low-cost wrapping material. Waxed paper often performs the same function at less cost than foil or plastic wrap. Also save reusable containers for storing foods in the refrigerator or freezer.

14. Avoid luxury foods such as snacks, convenience items, soft drinks, and ready-to-eat bakery products.

15. Be prepared to pay premium prices for specially packed dietetic foods.

16. Buy fresh foods that look fresh and are in good condition. It's a waste of time to cut away bad spots and a waste of money to throw away food.

17. When figuring the cost of a convenience food product, include the cost of all the ingredients you have to add.

18. Watch to see that the cashier rings up your purchases correctly—everyone makes an occasional mistake.

19. Make as few trips to the store as possible. Each trip means money spent for gas and another opportunity to buy unnecessary items that you may see.

FOOD STORAGE GUIDE

Because wasted food is wasted money, it's extremely important to store food properly. Be sure you unpack groceries promptly and store perishables as directed.

Eggs, cheese: Refrigerate eggs in the original carton or a covered container. Tightly cover and refrigerate cheese. To prevent the odor and flavor of strong cheeses from permeating other foods, store these cheeses in tightly covered jars.

Fresh fruits: Remove injured fruit and discard or use promptly. Ripen tomatoes, avocados, melons, peaches, pears, and plums at room temperature and out of direct sunlight; then refrigerate. Do not wash berries, cherries, or grapes until ready to serve. Store bananas and uncut pineapple in cool place. Refrigerate other fruits. If the fruit is purchased covered or in a plastic bag, make sure there are holes for air circulation. Remember, fresh fruits have a fairly short storage life.

Fresh vegetables: Store potatoes, dry onions, and winter squash in a cool, dry place; wash when ready to use. Wash and thoroughly drain greens, cabbage, carrots, celery, beets, radishes, and green onions (also remove excess tops); then refrigerate in separate moisture-vaporproof bags or airtight containers.

Fresh meat, poultry, fish: Loosely wrap fresh meat and poultry (wrap and store giblets separately), then refrigerate. Meats that are wrapped in clear plastic material when purchased can be refrigerated or frozen as is for 1 to 2 days. Remove paper wrappers from meat or poultry and rewrap with waxed paper before refrigerating. Use ground meat within 3 days, steaks and chops in 3 days, roasts in 5 to 6 days, whole poultry in 3 days, and cut-up poultry within 2 days.

Wrap fresh fish tightly in moisture-vaporproof material or seal in airtight container; refrigerate. Use in 2 days.

Canned goods: Store in cool, dry place.

Leftover food: Cool cooked food quickly, then cover and refrigerate. Refrigerate canned foods, covered, in original can. Cover egg yolks with cold water; refrigerate in a tightly covered container for up to 2 days. Refrigerate egg whites in tightly covered container up to 10 days.

COMMON CAN SIZES

Container	Approximate Net Weight or Fluid Measure	Cup Measure	Principal Foods
8 ounce	8 ounces	About 1 cup	Fruits, vegetables
Picnic	10½ to 12 ounces	About 1¼ cups	Condensed soups
12 ounce (vacuum)	12 ounces	About 1½ cups	Vacuum-packed corn
No. 300	14 to 16 ounces	About 1¾ cups	Baked beans, meats, spaghetti, macaroni, cranberry sauce
No. 303	16 to 17 ounces	About 2 cups	Fruits, vegetables, meats, ready-to-serve soups
No. 2	20 ounces	About 2½ cups	Juices, pie fillings, ready-to-serve soups
No. 2½	29 ounces	About 3½ cups	Fruits, pumpkin, sauerkraut, tomatoes
No. 3 cylinder or 46 fluid ounce	51 ounces (46 fluid ounces)	About 5¾ cups	Fruit and vegetable juices
No. 10	6½ to 7¼ pounds	12 to 13 cups	Institutional size

MAKE THE MOST OF MEATS

Meat accounts for the largest single expense in the food budget (about one-third). For this reason, wise buymanship, storage, and preparation are particularly important.

BUYING

The price of meat (remember to evaluate price per serving) is definitely one consideration of the budget-minded housewife. But don't settle for poor quality to save money. Learn which cuts are economical (see sketches, pages 91 and 92) and then choose good quality meat from these cuts.

Appearance is your best guide when selecting meat from the food store. Choose meat with a minimum amount of fat around the outer edges and with a good red color. This indicates good quality and freshness.

STORING

The most important rule for storing meat is to refrigerate or freeze it promptly. For refrigerator storage, see page 89.

Before freezing meat, divide it into family-sized portions and wrap it in a moisture-vaporproof material, such as clear plastic wrap, freezer-weight foil, or laminated wrap. It's important to freeze foods quickly, so place unfrozen foods in a single layer in the coldest part of your freezer. Make sure that the freezer temperature stays below 0°. Plan to use small meat cuts within 4 to 6 months and larger cuts within 8 to 12 months. Once completely thawed, never refreeze foods.

You can also freeze cooked meats. Be sure to chill the meat first. There's no need to thaw before reheating the meat.

PREPARING

The main thing to do when preparing meat is to use the right cooking method—tender meats are cooked with dry heat (roast, broil, panbroil, panfry), while less tender meats require moist heat (braise, cook in liquid). Most economy meat cuts fall in the moist-heat cooking category.

HOW MUCH MEAT TO BUY		
Food	**Form**	**Servings Per Pound**
Meat (beef, pork, veal, lamb)	With large amount of bone (ribs, shank) With medium amount of bone (chuck roast) With minimum amount of bone (steaks, roasts) Boneless or ground (canned ham, ground beef)	1 to 2 servings 2 to 3 servings 3 to 4 servings 4 servings
Chicken	Broiling Frying, roasting, stewing	1½ servings 2 servings
Turkey	5- to 12-pound size 12- to 24-pound size	1 to 1½ servings 1½ to 2 servings
Fish	Whole Dressed Steaks, Fillets Canned	1 to 1½ servings 2 servings 3 servings 5 servings

ECONOMICAL MEAT CUTS

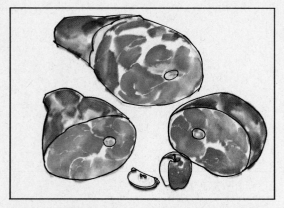

From upper left: *Shank ham half; butt ham half; picnic shoulder. Cook in liquid or roast all three.*

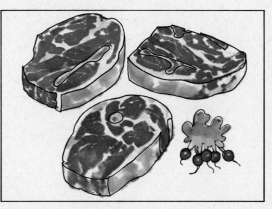

From upper left: *Beef pot roasts or steaks—flat-bone blade, 7-bone blade, arm. Braise all three.*

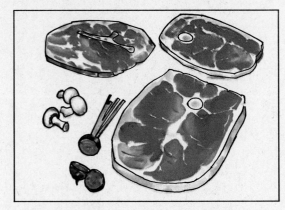

From upper left: *Pork blade steak; pork arm steak; beef round steak. Braise or panfry all three.*

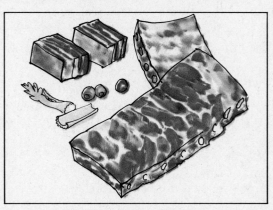

From top: *Beef short ribs—braise or cook in liquid; pork country-style ribs—roast or braise.*

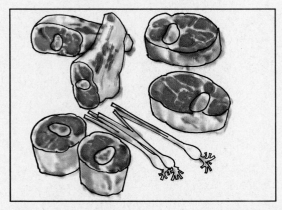

From upper left: *Lamb shanks; crosscut beef shanks; pork hocks. Cook in liquid or braise all three.*

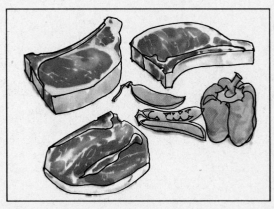

From top: *Pork rib chops; pork blade chop or steak. Braise or panfry both of these cuts.*

THREE-MEAL MEATS

CUTTING POULTRY

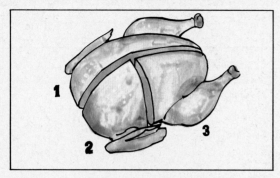

Have your meatman cut a turkey as shown. Freeze separately till needed, then roast. Serve **(1)** sliced. Use **(2)**, mostly white, and **(3)**, mostly dark, cubed or ground in sandwiches, casseroles, loaves.

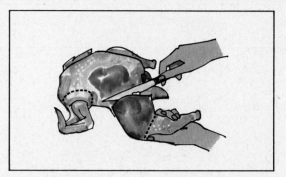

Cut skin between thigh and body. Pull leg away from body and cut between hip joint and body. Cut at knee joint. Pull wing away from body and cut at joint as shown by dots. Repeat for other leg and wing.

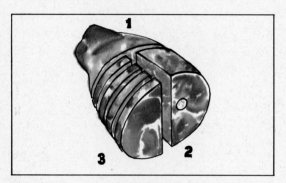

Stretch a 7-pound shank ham half by cutting it as shown. Use **(1)** section for soup or a boiled dinner. Serve **(2)** section baked with a sauce or glaze. Fry **(3)** slices or cube and use in casseroles.

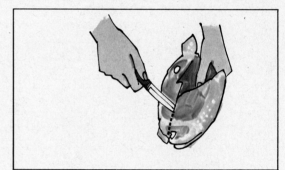

Place body of the bird, neck end down. Divide body by cutting along the breast end of the ribs to the neck as shown by dots. Repeat on other side. Cut through joints to separate breast and back.

Buy a 5- to 6-pound arm pot roast and cut it as shown. Freeze until needed. Bake the steaks from **(1)** section in a well-seasoned sauce. Pot-roast **(2)** section. Cube **(3)** and use as stew meat.

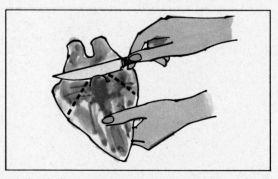

To divide breast into two pieces, use sharp paring knife to cut around bottom end of breastbone following curve of bones. For back, bend back in half to break at joint; cut to separate into two pieces.

INDEX